DIARY *of a* FatGirl

HOW I LOST 140 POUNDS, OVERCAME BINGE EATING DISORDER, AND LEARNED TO LOVE MYSELF AFTER WEIGHT LOSS SURGERY

Lisa Sargese

Publishing services provided by:

 Archangel Ink

ISBN-13: 9781450565561
ISBN: 1450565565

Contents

Foreword

CONSIDER THIS BOOK A UNIQUE experience. This book is an invitation to the inner heart and mind of Lisa. It feels like a tryst into the secret world of addiction, despair, and the ecstasy of rebirth.

As a certified hypnotist and master contemplative instructor, I am privileged to work with wonderful people and visit with their minds. For the past twenty years, I have witnessed true transformations with the very simple and God-given techniques of personal reflection. I met Lisa when she was pursuing her second Master's degree, and I had always been impressed with her keen insights and quick wit. When she asked me to work with her to prepare her for gastric bypass surgery for weight loss, I was delighted to help. Since I had worked in hospital settings before, I knew that hypnosis could be a powerful tool for healing and that it could make Lisa's outcome significantly better. I worked with her before the surgery to prepare her mind and body for the procedure and after it to focus her on recovery. I approached Lisa's gastric bypass surgery's pre– and post-operative sessions as a holistic journey from the past to the future freedoms and perceived gains that it promised. The sessions served as a bridge to mastery that must go through the four stages before the person truly feels able to make permanent cognitive-behavioral change. This work, based on neuroscience, allowed Lisa to survive a surgery that killed another patient her same age and size that very same day in another hospital. Her recovery was quick, and she reported feeling more energy than she had in years.

However, while I *know* that the mental-rehearsal procedure was a medical success, the imagery Lisa created in those few hypnotic sessions of the life she imagined having in the future was *not* enough to permanently ground her in the present for the year after the surgery. She was unprepared for the day-to-day unraveling of layers and layers of emotions that the process of weight loss demands. Emotions translate into biochemicals in the body that need to be shed via tears, laughter, and even physical pain. In this book, Lisa shares those moments as she aimed to create a new life of balance and an environment that fosters a strong sense of self or ego. Ego strengthening is a key and vital element to creating resilience and new behavior. This is not easy. It takes courage. Lisa shows you with humor and candor how she gained balance and harnessed personal courage.

Diary of a Fat Girl allows the reader entry into the innermost thoughts and feelings of a multifaceted, passionate, and deep life learner. With Lisa, you experience what true telepathy would feel like: to listen in and feel the flux of mental changes and insights. In her very raw and honest reflections, she permits an intimate and rich look into her very psyche (soul) such that you can palpate the elation and subsequent despair of being at once whole and complete, as well as flawed and vulnerable. This book will touch your heart by painting vivid imagery of what it is like to not trust your own body, even when your very own survival depends on trusting its intelligence.

Lisa takes us on a personal journey of discovery and revelation. She rolls out the players of her life: a self-involved mother, a distant yet caring father, an abusive live-in lover, and a full cast of powerful friends that guide her. She lets us see moments of awe and then moments of jealousy or fear.

As a mind/body professional, I witnessed firsthand the unveiling of the stages of change in Lisa's process in conjunction with this very special cast of friends, family, strangers, and angels. According to the research by contemplative scholars, most of us give up early in our efforts to change. Given the added layer of invasive and taxing surgeries that Lisa experienced, giving up might have been expected. However, she shows us that for those courageous enough to continue on, efforts to change and grow can lead to a life of mental contemplation and personal agency that allows us to re-create our lives and even our basic instincts. We can permanently change our personal script of how our lives were supposed to be. It is this tantalizing secret nod that Lisa's story offers. How can you change your life through self-reflection and raw honesty? What might you gain if you dared it?

Lisa reminds us that we are not alone in the world when we stare into the mirror, wondering if this is all there is. This book is a *must* for anyone who looks to go beyond their past experiences of blame, fear, or doubt and move boldly into self-discovery and its subsequent reawakening.

—Esmilda Abreu-Hornbostel, PhD
Founder and Director of NeuroLink Institute
New Milford, New Jersey

To see how I'm doing now and for plenty of free tools for your own success, visit LisaSargese.com

Find me on Instagram, Facebook, Twitter, and Tumblr for daily insights and inspiration so you can feel healthy and free!

Introduction

THIS IS MY STORY OF the first year following gastric bypass surgery. It is not an endorsement of weight-loss surgery, nor is it a warning against weight-loss surgery. It is my experience as I lived it, day-by-day, for one year of my life, during which time I lost 140 pounds.

The pages of this book are taken from my blog, which I began in August 2006 when I had the gastric bypass. In 2007, I pledged to blog every day in order to track my progress. Since then I have never missed a day—even when I had three surgeries to repair my knees, vacationed, or just didn't feel like it. I promised to blog every day, and I blogged.

I had my first weight-loss surgery when I was twenty-five years old. I weighed three hundred pounds and was suffering from a severe binge eating disorder. My first weight-loss surgery was an adjustable gastric banding performed by the pioneer surgeon Dr. Lubomyr Kuzmak. Today, the band is called a "lap band," because the surgery to install it is done laparoscopically. My surgery was not laparoscopic. My banding was an open, full-incision surgery. The band had to be replaced four years after installation. That second surgery was also a full-incision, open surgery. I have the railroad scar down my abdomen to show for it. In my blog, I talk about a third surgery to replace a defective portion of the band. I am sad to say that I don't remember if I underwent a third surgery. Depression, strong antidepressant drugs, and other factors make that portion of my life a hazy blur. Since Dr. Kuzmak has passed and the hospital no longer exists, it would be difficult to verify. The fact that I had two gastric banding surgeries is definite, as is my difficulties living a banded life.

My story involves many factors that led to my eating disorder, body dysmorphic disorder, and multiple surgeries, including being raised by a mother who suffered from narcissistic personality disorder. I was bullied from grammar school to middle school, suffered major depression, had a debilitating motor vehicle accident, and many troubled relationships. There may be one, some, or many situations with which you may identify, or maybe you will identity with none. It's important to me that I tell my story, because there is a chance that someone will feel less shamed, less isolated, and more empowered to seek help if they know they are not alone in their suffering.

When I say I suffered from a severe binge eating disorder, I mean to say I could eat a tremendous amount of food, often without purging, in order to punish myself and pass out. Love of food had nothing to do with my eating disorder. After the first bite the pleasure would end. Eating was a race to the finish. I was trying to finish myself. Food was merely my drug of choice.

When I say I could eat a tremendous amount of food, I mean I could devour two whole pizzas, three Entenmann's cakes, and a two-liter bottle of soda in a three-hour binge. That was extreme. Not every binge was that voluminous. Sometimes all it took were four peanut butter and jelly sandwiches and a can of soda to knock me out.

At the time, there was not much literature on binge eating disorder and there was no Internet. Eating disorders were characterized by eating too little. If one ate too much, one was sent to Overeaters Anonymous. I did attend the meetings but could not work the program. I believed I was a hopeless addict, but I was not without hope altogether. I figured I could decrease the damage of my binge eating by decreasing the size of my stomach. I had heard of someone getting their stomach stapled, so off to the library I went in search of information on this possible solution to my eating problem. That's how I found out about gastric banding. There was no Internet, but there were newspapers and magazines. I pursued the surgery with gusto.

I lost one hundred pounds during my first banded year. I vomited after every meal. I thought I had found my solution. I could still eat food, swallow food, but once it hit the stricture caused by the gastric band it would come up forcibly, sometimes through my nose. I didn't care. I had my drug of choice and a foolproof way to keep from suffering the consequences of weight gain, but there was a consequence of vomiting so often. The band dug into my stomach and had to be replaced. The second band malfunctioned. I was too poor and exhausted to go through a third surgery, so the malfunctioning band was left in. I was able to eat almost normally, which meant I gained back all the lost weight plus another hundred pounds. I think my highest weight was 420. I couldn't be sure as scales didn't go up that high back then.

It was at my highest weight that I sought another surgical solution. I still suffered a severe binge eating disorder and still believed a smaller stomach would solve my problem. By that time Dr. Kuzmak had passed away. It was difficult to find a surgeon who would take down the gastric band and convert it to a bypass, but I did. That is where this story begins. It took almost two hundred pages to tell the story of my first year after the gastric bypass; therefore, this book will be the first in a series. Recovery is not a straight road from sick to well. The road zigs and zags, is full of detours, roadblocks, and back tracks, but rest assured I've never stopped moving. I'm a fighter. I fight to win.

July 15, 2006

Starting with the Skim Milk

It all started with the skim milk.
Deprivation leads to bingeing—a lifetime of it.

I'VE ALWAYS WANTED TO BE lean, strong, and healthy. Well, sorta. A more honest statement would be: I've always wanted to be thin and pretty.

I dress it up in the more respectable phrase "lean, strong, and healthy." That's what I would recommend to a client, or student, or friend. I would recommend that if they wanted to lose weight, they should lose weight and get in shape for the sake of their health and well-being, not for someone else's approval. I would try to convince them that "if you have your health, you have everything" (or however that old saying goes).

But when it comes to describing the motivation for my own dreams and my own goals, if I say I'm doing it for my health, I'm full of crap. The truth is, I want to be thin and pretty. Why? Maybe I'm shallow. Maybe that's the only way I'll feel socially acceptable.

Or maybe I'm scarred.

When someone suffers repeated, systematic abuse as a child, they're scarred. The unmet need for approval runs deep. Being scarred is no excuse for bad behavior, but is trying to become thin and pretty really bad behavior? I teach religion and women's studies, so you can imagine that blogging about wanting to be thin and pretty is problematic. As I teach my students, it's time to unpack the backstory.

'Too fat' was the first criticism I remember receiving. It was the first not-good-enough that stung. I don't remember being 'wrong' or 'bad' about anything prior to my pediatrician telling my mother I was over- weight and to switch me over to skim milk. Did he ask about my activity level? I don't remember. Did he recommend more fruits, vegetables or lean protein? Not that I recall. He probably meant to suggest a minor change in diet. Since this was 1969 and kids drank big glasses of milk with every meal, he probably saw his suggestion to switch to skim milk as a practical recommendation to cut a percentage of fat out of my diet, but that's not what my mother heard. What she heard was that she was an imperfect mother with a flawed daughter that cast an unfavorable light on her.

With his off-hand skim milk recommendation he started my mother down a slippery slope of imposed deprivation, body shaming, and dieting that contributed to my developing an eating disorder that started with sneak eating in my childhood to binge eating in adulthood. Worse yet, the skim milk didn't do anything for my weight issue. I remained chubby for my age. My mother stepped up her game.

She embarrassed me publicly. At social functions, while the other kids were enjoying dessert, she would openly, loudly announce that I was on a diet and was not allowed to have any treats. I sat there feeling like a freak, watching the other kids eat. If I sulked or showed any kind of disappointment, my mother would again embarrass me by asking me, openly and loudly, if I wanted to be fat like one of Cinderella's ugly stepsisters and if so, then I should *go ahead* and have dessert. Even though I wanted the dessert and I wanted to join in with the other kids, I would put my head down in mortification. Having defeated me she would announce to everyone, "*See? She doesn't want to be fat and ugly!*" My show of willpower made her feel good, because she believed it was evidence that she was an exemplary mother. Kids and parents looked at me with a mix of pity and aversion. She made me an outcast who was sometimes mistaken for a snob. That "specialness" spilled over to the way she controlled my social habits. I wasn't permitted to casually play with other children. Play visits were prearranged and supervised. They always took place at our house. On the rare occasions that I was allowed to visit a friend's home for play time or a birthday party, my mother would walk me to the door and tell the parent that I was not allowed to have any snacks, desserts, or birthday cake because the doctor had put me on a diet. The parents didn't enforce this but I was too obedient to try to defy my mother's control.

While the other kids enjoyed cake or ice cream or, God forbid, a piece of candy, they would look at me with squinted eyes, wondering why I wasn't doing what they were all doing. I sat there empty-mouthed and empty-handed, watching them eat and feeling left out.

Sometimes the adults took pity on me and told me it was a special occasion, that it was alright to have "just a little piece." I would refuse, not out of discipline, but out of fear of my mother. She would grill me after the visit. She would put me on the spot and ask if I had indulged in any of the forbidden food. I always reported that I had refused all offers of food. I believe I *did* slip up one time. I remember it vaguely. One of the mothers had convinced me to have "just a little piece," and I did. The other mother was an adult after all, an authority figure. If my friend's mother said it was all right, then it must be. I wanted a piece of cake so bad. I ate some.

When I admitted this to my mother during her post-visit questioning, she became enraged. How dare I let some other woman override her edict. What was the matter with me? Who the hell was so-and-so's mother to give me permission to eat cake? Did I want to go live with *those* people instead? Since I was willing to listen to so-and-so's mother, I must be unhappy living with my own Mommy and Daddy and my cat, so I should go live with those other people if that's who I was going to listen to. She always threatened abandonment. She hollered at me. Sometimes she'd hit me—never enough to leave a mark, just hard enough to humiliate me and establish her dominance.

In spite of all that imposed deprivation in and out of my household, I was still chubby. Back in the day, we ate Arnold's or Pepperidge Farm white bread, bologna and cheese sandwiches, peanut butter and jelly, SpaghettiOs, sugary cereals, steaks with butter, hot dogs, cheeseburgers—all in the name of the four food groups and the all-American diet. The food I ate was very tightly portion-controlled but also processed, fatty, and starchy. And I was sedentary. I was not permitted to work up a sweat. I was not permitted to run around outside with the other kids. I was not allowed to make noise. According to my mother, only "common" kids ran around and made noise like commoners and animals. No daughter of hers was going to run around like a common animal.

For much of my childhood at home I was silent, sedentary, and so hungry. The small portions of food I ate for breakfast and lunch were not filling. The processed-carbohydrate content of most of my breakfast and lunchtime foods gave me energy highs then dropped me down in the low blood sugar pits. My stomach growled before every meal.

I was so hungry by the time we sat down to dinner. I always felt starving and anxious at the dinner table. My parents bickered and sniped at each other. My father was hungry and grouchy after his day at work. His highball cocktails before supper either brightened his mood or made him defensive against my contentious, critical mother. During dinner I always had the feeling that they could explode at any moment. I ate in fear.

I wolfed down my food in a hurry. I wanted to be able to put away my first round of meat, potatoes, and vegetables and grab a giant helping of seconds before my parents were finished eating or started fighting, thereby signaling the end of dinnertime. It was a race to get my needs met. My father scolded me for eating so much so fast. He accused me of making noises like a pig when I ate. It must have sounded that way as I gulped and scarfed my food. I often had the hiccups.

I was five years old when all this started. The humiliation. The deprivation. The dieting. I was suffering and blamed myself for my pain. I reasoned that I was somehow bad and that was why I felt so hurt all the time. At five years old, I understood that if I were thin and pretty, the doctor would *never* have recommended the switch to skim milk. I was convinced that my suffering was my fault for not being what I was supposed to be: a doll for my mother to parade around in order to receive attention and praise. As a chubby girl, I attracted too much criticism. The criticism landed on her. Therefore, I needed to be perfected so that my mother could feel superior. If I could be thin and pretty, I could be loved and all would be well.

July 17, 2006

CHOCOLATE CAKE FOR LUNCH

TODAY I HAD CHOCOLATE CAKE for lunch. Well, it's not like that's *all* I had for lunch. I had a slice of room temperature pizza first, then had the chocolate cake. I felt terrible about it. I'm so tired of feeding myself. I'm tired of being hungry. My stomach feels like a greedy furnace, always wanting to be filled. It's never satisfied. I want to be free of this demanding monster.

I had an appointment with my bariatric surgeon today, but he was delayed in NYC, where he has his main practice, and I have been "pushed back" to Friday at 9:30 a.m. I'm counting the minutes till I am on the operating table getting my Roux-en-Y (RNY) gastric bypass. I want to be free.

July 18, 2006

A BINGE

I EAT BECAUSE MY STOMACH feels empty. I fill it, but I'm still empty. I eat until it hurts. I eat till the food inside me feels like a hunk of lead trying to pound its way out of me from the inside. I stuff myself till I'm preoccupied with the pain. The emotional emptiness that made me overeat in the first place becomes a weak, abstract notion at the periphery of my consciousness. All that exists is the fullness, the pounding, the heavy distraction of too much food, killing me.

July 22, 2006

Transamerica and the Flat Abs of the Irrepressible Sydney

I JUST WATCHED THE FILM *Transamerica*. I feel like Bree (Felicity Huffman) counting the days till I go under the knife. She told her therapist (Elizabeth Peña) that the day of her sexual reassignment surgery would be the happiest day of her life. I understand. Bree corrected her son, who mistakenly referred to the sexual reassignment surgery as "having her dick cut off," by telling him it was more like having it turned inside out. It made me think of my gastric bypass surgery. It's not like a way to get all this fat cut off, but a way of turning myself inside out. At forty-two, it's time for my insides to match my outside. I'm ready to love myself skinny.

In the film, Bree's pretty sister, Sydney (Carrie Preston), is a lithe, blonde beauty with a dynamite shape. I was supposed to be watching Felicity Huffman giving her Oscar-worthy performance, but when Preston was on the screen I couldn't take my eyes off her abs—sexy, flat, youthful abs. Love-worthy abs. I felt grotesque, like a misshapen lump.

Why was I comparing myself to her? How self-destructive. How awful of me. I should love myself just the way I am, right? What a load of crap. Bree couldn't love that part of herself that made her biologically male. Looking at her spunky sister, braless and buoyant with those irrepressible abs, made me hate the part of me that makes me fat.

I check Preston's bio on a few sites. No birth year. I'll hazard a guess she's between thirty-five and forty-five. I found a beautiful picture of her on the red carpet in a stunning black gown, her left ring finger flashing a diamond ring. I believe that's how I have to look to be one of those red-carpet ladies or one of those ring-sporting ladies who get to show the world that someone loves them enough to buy them a big fat diamond. The skinny gets the ring.

I feel like a blob, yet I know that's wrong-headed. I bear the burden of summoning love for my blob of a self. I'm the one who has to pull myself up out of this fat vat and make myself into a figure that I can love. It's quite a paradox, having to love the unlovable in order to make myself feel deserving of love. Maybe I should buy myself a ring.

July 25, 2006
Too Fat to Enfold

Is it because I'm too big that there are no arms to comfort me? I try to use my own arms but they can't reach around me, not to my satisfaction. I can't hug myself with arms, so I'm hugging myself inside this fat. The fat is the embrace that shields me from the world. Food is the false comfort that makes me even larger and all the less huggable. They say I should go on a big beautiful woman (BBW) dating site and find a guy who likes big girls. No fetishy fat-lover will do. It's me that needs the comfort, the holding, not someone's body preference with the rest of me as merely incidental. By the time I shed the fat, I may be self-sufficient. If I'm skinny in my dream body, I might not need to be held. If the holding comes, it will come too late and may seem inauthentic, a consequence of the skinny rather than true affection. I crave the ideal embrace that no one can give me, not now at least, not until I've embraced myself—differently.

July 27, 2006

STOMACH FUCKER

I'M TIRED OF BEING A trooper. Can't I just be a coward and let people go easy on me? Do I always have to be so strong? Passive, suffering, but strong?

I had my upper endoscopy today, part of my pre-op testing for my upcoming RNY gastric bypass. The anesthesiologist poked me three times with a needle, trying to find a vein so he could administer twilight anesthesia that would put me under. My shy veins rolled and receded, refusing to let him insert the IV needle that would twilight-anesthetize me for the procedure. He seemed impatient, as if finding a vein was taking too long. He said that he didn't want to keep sticking me with the needle like that, and would I mind just having a throat-numbing local anesthetic and staying awake for the procedure. He assured me that he, himself, had undergone the same procedure that way and that he would be "with me" the whole time during mine.

Now, a sane, reasonable person would imagine that the discomfort of an awake-endoscopy would be less severe than being pricked over and over by an IV needle, right? Or else he wouldn't have offered, right? So I consented . . . to what turned out to be one of the most traumatic experiences of my life. A nurse strapped a mouthpiece over my face so I could bite down on it while it provided the gastroenterologist with an opening into which he would insert the scope, a thick, pliant tube with a camera at the end.

The anesthesiologist and the nurse held me down as I lay on my side on the gurney. From the moment the doctor inserted that tube down my throat, I wretched and heaved in an involuntary spasm of convulsive vomiting while the nurse and anesthesiologist told me to *breathe*, which, I imagine, is as useless as telling a woman in labor to *push*.

The doctor plunged and withdrew and plunged and withdrew the scope. It felt like a giant garden hose invading me over and over again while I heaved, my body attempting to reject the violent, penetrating object. My stomach spasmed. I puked sticky saliva out of my nose and the corners of my mouth while I tried to remove my consciousness from my body. I couldn't help thinking about *House M.D.* and how those poor patients often suffer through invasive tests when it looks as if they could easily be put under some sort of sedative to lessen the trauma. I told myself that if they could endure, so could I. Time slowed down relentlessly. "Forty-five more seconds, you're doing great!" they assured me. I tried to count backward. *Ten, nine, eight, seven* . . . I didn't think I could tolerate the invasion any longer. My stomach was convulsing, trying to expel the tube that was all the way down my esophagus. I was vomiting but couldn't get rid of what needed to come up, because the doctor was shoving it down into me. I wanted to reach up and push the doctor away from me. My instinct was to grab his necktie and pull it like an emergency brake on a train. I wanted him to stop. Dear God, how was such suffering possible? I grabbed the polished chrome railing of the gurney instead.

When he finally finished and mercifully withdrew the monster scope, they unstrapped the mouthpiece. I gasped for air and shook for a moment, then started to cry.

The nurse who had held me down during the procedure gave me tissues and looked at me with kindness and sympathy. She wanted to know why I was crying.

August 3, 2006
Even the Mirror Wouldn't Tell Me

I 'M ALWAYS SHOCKED BY pictures of myself. How did I get to be this big? I'm approaching four hundred pounds. Funny, when I weighed under 185 pounds—pretty, buxom, just a bit pudgy—I thought I was fat and disgusting. Now, I feel like I really am fat and disgusting, and I go around with a false image of myself as being merely a bit pudgy. I believed I was just a bit pudgy, until my blood sugar started hitting the six-hundred range and I saw a picture of myself standing next to a thin person. I was almost three times their size.

"Oh noooo," folks will say, "you have to love yourself just the way you are" or, "It's not what's on the outside that makes you beautiful." Ah, yes. Small consolation for the unacceptably obese is that we can be "good people." Pretty on the inside. Dangerously fat and unwanted everywhere else.

How did I get this big? I stood in front of the mirror and dared to tell myself that I was "OK" just as I am. By getting on with substantial aspects of life other than my looks, by succeeding at things other than being thin, I'm OK. I'm a university professor. I'm active in student affairs. I lead an eating and body image support group. I'm about to finish up my second Master's degree. I'm a private tutor. I have an eBay business. I do stuff. I do it well. That should make me OK, right?

All this time it was easy to deny that I was becoming grotesquely obese because positive reinforcement came in response to my intellectual endeavors and my social-justice activities. Academe is a strange land with strange-looking people roaming about, garnering respect for their accomplishments regardless of their often antisocial appearance. How was I supposed to know that I was becoming less and less socially acceptable due to my size when people were treating me with respect? I figured I was "OK." Who was going to tell me that I was freakishly huge?

No one was rude enough to tell me, except my father and my best friend—and I didn't want to believe them.

August 6, 2006

Happy Birthday, Fat Girl

Today is my forty-second birthday.

Happy birthday, fat girl! For all the pounds of empty calories consumed in hopes of finding that sweet spot between loved and satisfied . . . in hope that sugar loses its sweetness in favor of the sweet sumptuousness of creativity and accomplishment . . . in spite of the greasy tomboys and assorted bullies who called you names and terrorized you in gym class . . . in acknowledgement for all the steadfast tolerance of well-meaning friends and family who said all the wrong things and pushed all your most sensitive buttons with their overly simplistic sideline cries of "don't blow it" and "just use your willpower" when you know more than anyone how much willpower it takes to walk out that front door into a hostile, judgmental world where "no fat chicks" is a T-shirt mantra worn by the male-mediocre . . . for all those outfits that you wore simply because the only clothes made in your size look like they should cover a couch rather than a human body . . . wishing you peace to replace the anguish of being overlooked in favor of your slim girlfriends who dragged you into public party places despite your protests . . . in sympathy for all the smiling and inconspicuous drink holding you did while others danced, flirted, and made out with cute boys who looked past you as if you weren't there . . . for all the celebrity crushes and real-life crushes you had that gave you emotional recreation, pain, joy, and companionship when their basis in reality was nearly baseless . . . in recognition of all your protestations that you really weren't interested in meeting anyone or dating or socializing because you were busy with school, work, writing, art, the Internet and anything else that wouldn't put you in the position to be hurt, judged, or told "I bet that in every class you were in, you were always the fattest one" . . . in expectation of becoming healthy inside and out and loving of yourself in all your incarnations . . . and of shaking the dust from your feet of all the hurtful, unappreciative, insensitive, ugly experiences that have fooled you into thinking you were anything less than a miracle, a genius, a reflection of divine perfection, and downright entitled to abundant joy in a universe of infinite love and possibility designed especially for your pleasure.

Happy birthday, fat girl . . . may you feel the warm embrace of total acceptance in your year of transformation . . . may you overcome, persevere, and triumph in the face of overwhelming odds that seem to be stacked against you . . . may you be free from the yoke of self-doubt . . . free from self-imposed limits . . . free from the cutthroat jealousy of others who feel uncomfortable about your blossoming...be free, be free to bloom...free to expand spiritually while you shed the pounds of old armor that dragged you along, earthbound and defeated...may you be free and buoyant, beautiful and beloved as you were meant to be.

August 14, 2006

STEP ONE: DEFLATE

I'M EXCITED. THEY'RE GOING TO slay my dragon Wednesday morning. The greedy, angry, fire-breathing furnace will be separated from my esophagus . . . forever. Is this a quick fix? Nah. Not by a long shot.

People say that having weight-loss surgery is taking the easy way out. Easy? I'm no stranger to weight-loss surgery. I had the adjustable gastric band operation back in 1989. I was one of the first in the nation to have the Kuzmak band installed. It worked beautifully as an induced bulimia device. They sold me the idea of gastric banding by saying I would be "full" and "sated" once the little pouch of my banded stomach filled up with two ounces of food. That's not how it happened. What happened? The first sip of liquid or the first bite of food, no matter how pureed, would hit the little opening between the banded pouch and my stomach and *hurt* like hell as I jumped up and down, burped, and vomited to try to get it to go through to my stomach. Eventually the dancing, burping, and vomiting routine would stretch the band enough to allow a meager meal to get through. Most of the time, I just ate and puked. The puking was easy. It happened automatically.

I lost one hundred pounds. I also irritated, swelled, and scarred up my stomach so badly, the band could no longer be loosened from the outside and they had to reoperate. They installed a new gastric band. It never worked. The new band sprang a leak. They needed to replace it. I threw my hands in the air. Not another surgery. Not another full incision. No more gutting me like a mother sturgeon about to have her delicious caviar stolen in a lethal, forced abortion.

Of course, everyone thought the defective band was my own fault. I had defeated the surgery somehow. No one acknowledged the lie of satiety or the possibility that the band might have been placed incorrectly inside me to begin with.

Almost twenty years later I'm going in to have the band removed and revised to a gastric bypass. After many failed diets and impossible exercise routines; after criticism and demeaning, unwanted advice; after pain in my knees, feet, and back and the consequent immobility; after being rejected by four surgeons who thought my scar tissue was "too complicated" to deal with, I'm going in for my lifesaving surgery.

A quick fix? You've got to be kidding.

How about a long-term fix? Heck, look at Carnie Wilson. She's on Celebrity Fit Club because she's regained a good portion of her weight after undergoing gastric bypass surgery in 1998. She's like me—a compulsive, emotional, and recreational eater. One must fix the head if the gut fix is to work. I think I'm doing plenty to deal with the nonphysical realm of my healing.

I know it's not going to be easy, but livin' ain't easy anyway.

For every failure story there's a triumph story. Who's to say I won't be the one who takes the weight off, keeps it off, and gets famous in the process? Who's to say I won't find the best way to make this work so I can help others get the most out of this surgery?

Who's to say this isn't the magic bullet?

I'll decide if it's the magic bullet or not. Shoot me. I'm getting well.

August 16, 2006

Day of the Gastric Bypass Surgery

THERE'S A MERMAID IN THE ICU

I WAS CALM GOING IN. In fact, I was downright blissful. The pre-op nurses were visiting me in my curtained-off area just to sit on the edge of my bed and chat with me. "She was hypnotized!" they told each other. Indeed, I was. My pre-op hypnosis involved two forty-five-minute sessions during which suggestions were implanted in my subconscious mind dictating the ease and success of my gastric bypass surgery. The hypno-counselor created calming associations for all the beeping, needling, brightly lit, cold sensations that accompany a trip to the operating room. Every noise, all the pokes and prods, the fussing of all the nurses in their scrubs just made me smile and relax more and more. I lay there on the gurney with a dopey grin. I had no worries. Success was imminent. I was certain.

Five and a half hours later, I awoke with a tube in my neck, a chest full of sticky heart monitor pads, a bruised abdomen, and pain—lots of pain—but I was still grinning. I was alive! "We're taking you to ICU. Your blood sugar was too high on the table and your red blood cell count is too low. We need to keep an eye on you, OK?" Sure, it's OK. Who was talking to me, anyway? And what was that burning, throbbing . . . *ouch!* "Here's your morphine. Just press this button!" Ah, it must have been the voice of an angel I was hearing. I pressed the magic button and let the warm rush of painlessness wash over me as I relaxed.

Except for my legs. They wouldn't keep still. I couldn't resist the urge to point my toes and kick my legs like I was swimming. Kick, point, kick, point, ballet, ballet, ballet. The nurses were entertained. One of them asked if I had "restless leg syndrome." The other nurse told her that I was moving because I was determined not to get clots and *that's* why I was twizzling my legs in the air in my ever so stylish disposable hospital booties. But really, it was an uncontrollable urge and I couldn't stop. Hypnotic suggestion, perhaps? Or was my inner mermaid trying to get out?

August 17, 2006

I SHIT THE BED. DIARRHEA seeped out of me uncontrollably, immersing me hip deep in humiliation. Thankfully, I was in the ICU, where shit and trembling are everyday occurrences for the nursing staff. I sobbed and apologized while the nurse and her assistant worked swiftly to clean me and make the bed with me still in it. I whimpered and apologized incessantly. The nurse reassured me that my accident was a blessing. "Most of the patients here in intensive care don't even realize they've had an accident. At least you're well enough to know that it happened."

Cleaned and powdered, hooked up to wires and beeping monitors, I drifted off to sleep, grateful for my shitty life.

October 7, 2006

Pureed Chicken Makes Me Gag

The smell of pureed chicken made me gag. It's worse than cat food. It's worse than dog food. But the hospital kitchen insisted on putting it on my tray, day after day. No matter how I complained, and I did complain, there it was, stinking to high heaven, making me gag. I was despondent. I called the kitchen. I talked to the impatient dietetics person on the other end of the line who sighed with exasperation and told me, "You're on a doctor-prescribed diet. Talk to your nurse!" So I reasoned with her, "What if I was vegetarian? Would you still send me pureed meat?" and she'd relent. Whoever was on staff would agree that there was something else I was entitled to eat and instead of pureed, stinking chicken, they'd send me a blob of pureed vegetable, equally unappealing but without the smell.

I had already been in the hospital twice as long as expected, mostly in the ICU. My blood sugar was out of control in the operating room, so I was on IV antibiotics and insulin. By the time I was transferred to a normal room, I had been living on ice chips for days. I was hungry. Even with a thimble-sized pouch of a stomach, I wanted to eat. Even with a teeny tiny pouch of a stomach, I was nauseated to the point of dry heaves by the smell of pureed chicken and there it was on my tray, stinking at me.

I bitched, I moaned, I buzzed the nurse. A registered dietician came to visit me in my room. She shamed me. She told me I was on a doctor-prescribed diet and to stop making such a fuss. I persisted. She checked the "manifest" and discovered that in the pureed stage of my eating gulag I was permitted to have strained cream soup, cottage cheese, broth, *V8* juice, Jell-O, yogurt, and sugar-free ice cream. I was hopeful. She left me with a promise of these runny delights and I waited eagerly for my next tray. Just as she promised, I had a miniature blob of cottage cheese, a nice little bowl of creamed, nondescript beige soup and a *V8*. Never had hospital food looked so good! I dove in and ate four spoonfuls. All that fighting and whining for four lousy spoonfuls.

The next day, the next tray, they sent me pureed chicken. The revolting smell assaulted me when I lifted the industrial plastic cover off my plate. Every other meal, it happened. I had to kick, scream, and fight for something edible to be sent to my room like I was fighting for the first time. I felt like I was singing for my supper, and sing I did. Sing, sing, sing, and then only able to eat four spoonfuls of whatever they deigned to send me. Never again, I told myself. I felt like Scarlett O'Hara, pulling puny turnips from the war-torn ground, screaming, "When I get out of here, I'll never go hungry again!"

October 16, 2006

Food's Gone

It's been weeks since I came home from the hospital feeling feverish, weak, and in pain. I'm still healing up after a rough surgery. I can barely eat.

The food's gone and so is my armor. Everything hits me directly, like I'm being pelted with feelings. I twitch. I shiver. I'm restless. I sleep well at night and am therefore deprived of naps during the day. There's no escape from my life.

It's a good life. Financially, I'm a little down, but that's to be expected for a grad student who only works part-time, and that work is play. Teaching religion and philosophy to college students, so young, so unjaded, not yet ruined by the pelting world. Hardly the nine-to-five grind.

I'm depressed. Not meaning I'm sad, though I am profoundly sad—sad over the state of the world, over the cruelty of humanity, over injustice and tragedy. Sad in a *big* way, but in a small way, in a chronic way, I'm depressed. Nothing makes me happy anymore. I like TV. My shows distract me from all the meaninglessness. Christian Troy and his antics. *Lost* and its mysteries. Dexter and his inability to resonate with society, plus all that killing. Nancy Botwin in *Weeds*. They provide me with temporary escape. What happened to me when I lost food? How did losing the over-stuffing, overeating, incapacitating gorging bring me to this state of grey? Beige? Bland like steamed diet food, blah at the world, lack of inspiration? I get full, but I can eat a lot. A whole package of that fake crab—sea legs, they call it? Pretzels by the handful. Raw peppers with tons of sea salt. One slice of protein bread with fat-free cheese. On paper it's not much. Under fifteen hundred calories in a day. Less than two grams of fat per meal or snack. I can't tolerate any fat. It nauseates me.

By volume, I'm not eating a lot—it just feels that way. I still crave the fullness, the uncomfortable fullness. Except now, I achieve it with a lot less food.

October 22, 2006

WHY WOULDN'T I WATCH TOO MUCH TV?

I DO. I DO WATCH too much TV. Hell, I should *be* on TV! But I'm not blaming myself. Blaming myself takes up too much time and too much energy. Too much, too much, too much? Too much.

That phrase, "too much" isn't helping me anymore. As a matter of fact, it never did. I've been blaming and chastising myself for years under the guise of self-discipline, but all it's done is make me feel like shit about myself. Too much. Enough.

My body hurts. Knees, back, joints, the site of the surgery. The side effects of morbid obesity. The body aches. Arthritis kicks in. Joint pain. Ouch.

So, yeah. I watch TV. It entertains me. It keeps me company. It inspires me to know what's possible beyond my four walls.

Project Runway delights me. Laura Bennett throwing her hands in the air saying, "I'm fabulously glamorous!" Jeffrey Sebelia claiming, "I got mad skills." Nancy in *Weeds* starting her own business. The patients on *Nip/Tuck* finally getting their excess flesh removed after drastic weight loss.

Yeah, I love TV, because for now, it doesn't hurt.

October 23, 2006
Picking at My Skin

I am a self-mutilator. I have been for many years, at least since puberty.

My mother taught me how to do it. She shamed me into it. She didn't know it would begin a lifelong habit of self-harm.

We were in the car, on our way to her brother's house—my beloved uncle, a sweet, funny, but judgmental man. My mother, from the driver's seat, told me to look in the visor mirror at my forehead. I had a small cluster of pimples, my first outbreak on an otherwise pristine face. She told me to squeeze the biggest one to get the pus out. She wanted to know why I hadn't noticed it on my own. I dug in with my fingernails and squeezed out a little blob of cottage-cheesy pus then wiped it on my jeans. She nodded in approval. Thus, it began.

My mirror became a backsplash for zits, a place to notice my flaws and get rid of them, a place to excise the bad feelings of inadequacy.

The next day at school, the innocent cluster of pimples was a flattened patch of scabs. They were dark and more noticeable than the zits had been, but cleaner in my mind—flat, empty, and clean. My teacher wanted to know how I had hurt myself. She looked concerned.

I'm not so bad about picking at my face, now. I'm self-conscious enough to avoid major digging and gouging at my face, though I still create tiny scabs when I "clean my pores." My crater making happens elsewhere now, under wraps, secretly. My breasts are covered with scabs. The stretched-out skin from the yo-yo weight gain and weight loss pulls my pores into grotesquely oversized holes that fill with baby powder, body cream, skin—a playground of squeezing.

During the worst of the diabetes, with blood sugars in the six hundreds, I gouged my way to a staph infection that nearly killed me. My body lost its ability to heal. The picked-at zits became open wounds, became boils, became carbuncles. I had to be hospitalized. It took three weeks on intravenous antibiotics to cure me. Every nurse who came into my hospital room to dress my gaping wounds told me that I was lucky to be alive.

All the docs and nurses assumed the holes in my skin just happened, that the diabetes made the craters. No one figured out that I was the one who made them, that I was the original cause of the holes, some three inches in diameter or more, all over my body. To them, it was my stubbornness, my refusal to manage my sugar that erupted into boils. They didn't ask about the holes. They figured they were sores that magically appeared. My secret was safe.

November 7, 2006

DAMAGE AND DAD

MY FATHER WAS HORRIFIED BY my appearance. He arrived before I did at my aunt and uncle's anniversary party at a semi-elegant catering hall. He was standing in the corner near the head table talking to my mother's brother. This party was for my mother's side of the family, and she wasn't there. They don't like her. Her public behavior is erratic and embarrassing. She makes scenes whenever she's at a family gathering. Everyone loves my dad. He's low-key, funny, easy to talk to. He gets along with everybody, except my mother; but then again, I'm one of the few people who can handle her. I handle her, but at the expense of my health. She doesn't understand how her loud, critical, abusive, and mostly unreasonable behavior is off-putting and inappropriate. *Forgive her, for she knows not what she does,* I tell myself. I don't forgive, but I tolerate. I run interference between her and her public victims. I've tried to tell her how she's damaged me. She just cries. She doesn't understand, so I bear the brunt of her mental illness, her narcissistic personality disorder. My dad just lives with her and suffers. He appeases her to keep her quiet. He looked the other way from the way she terrorized me as a child, because he didn't want to rock the boat and bring on any of her raging blowups.

He married her because she was a hot blonde who looked great riding in his 1956 Chevy convertible. True story. They met as she was getting out of an ugly divorce from an abusive man who micromanaged her life and their finances. My father, the least controlling man she'd ever met (and handsome and needy), had a large, loving family that offered her an escape from the outcast existence of a divorcée. Marrying my father was her way out of the inevitable return to her father's web of control out in California. My parents, two great-looking newlyweds, childless for nine years till I came along, married for all the wrong reasons.

But my father hasn't learned. He married a difficult shrew of a woman because she was pretty. Looks mean a lot to him, and I don't have them. Being smart but fat with a pretty face isn't immediately recognizable as attractive. I reflect on him poorly.

So, when I walked across the dance floor toward him, waddling under the weight of my excess fat, he looked panicked and ashamed. My slender, financially successful, married cousins, wispy in their satin dresses, flanked by their husbands and healthy, beautiful children, embodied the ideal that my father wanted for his daughter. I was not what he wanted: overweight, hopelessly single, overeducated, underemployed, childless, and wheezing from my crippling fat. The look of disapproval on his face was undeniable. I approached him and he embraced me dutifully. I greeted my aunts and uncles who were warm and conciliatory, understanding (and happy) that my mother stayed home. I joked that my father would have a much better time without her, but I carried her with me, the bulk of me, my internalized pain carried on my small frame for all to see, barely covered by the stretched-out material of the largest-size dress available from the fat-girl store. My father looked at me and frowned.

I sneaked out of the party before they served dessert.

November 13, 2006

I'm Melting

IT'S BEEN THREE MONTHS SINCE the gastric bypass. I'm shaped like melted Play-Doh. I'm not bouncing back, I'm just shrinking. My melty meatball shape is deflating and sagging toward the ground. I feel repulsive.

Imagine having to go out into the world in this saggy case I call a body. Imagine what it has been like waddling around like a bloated meatball for all these years. "Love yourself," people told me. "Love yourself. You have to love yourself first, or no one else will love you."

Love this? How?

"It's who you are inside that matters," they say. I say, bullshit. My insides matter? To whom? Who's getting past the outside to my insides? I've been used, abused, and taken advantage of by quite a few con artists, chronic misfits, and punishers looking to be superior to someone who has low self-esteem. They put me down to boost their own egos. Draining.

Now, I have a select group of dear friends. It took half a life to be able to detect and honor sincerity. I'm blessed to have some sincere friends.

My self-image has always relied on the nonphysical. Looking at myself has always been painful. I hated what I saw in the mirror. When I knew it was time to help my self-esteem and improve my health, I was forced to look at the truth in that mirror. Damage. Disaster.

Self-help books got me through the self-hate. Good enough, smart enough, and—doggone it—people like me, they preached. Tell yourself something long enough and you just might believe it. I told myself I was just fine the way I am, just perfect, a work in progress, lovable, beautiful, differently shaped. Big and round like the goddess. Fertile and spherical like the earth, I'd tell myself, but I didn't really believe it. I've been miserable. Crippled. Sick.

There is beauty in suffering. *Life* magazine photos of innocents crying with ruins in the background. War pictures of simple folks, sullen and desperate. Rescue missions. Bandaged soldiers. We honor our artists and photojournalists and writers for showing us the beauty of ugliness in the world. It jars us. We are disturbed and hopefully we act to change things.

Looking in the mirror, I feel like a *Life* magazine war scape. I look at my war-torn body, scabs, scars, stretch marks, and heavy sacks of fat that I wish would disappear. I try to tell myself I am beautiful. I rush to drape as much concealing fabric over the mess of flesh, politely covering the anathema of the too-muchness. I feel uglier than a war scape. Even *Life* magazine wouldn't publish a photo of me.

Part of me knows I have to fall in love with the ugly. I'm my own work of art wanting to change. I see beauty in potential, the potency of what could be.

November 25, 2006

NE'ER-DO-WELL EX-BOYFRIEND

HE PRETENDED TO LOVE ME. Maybe he really thought he loved me. I thought he loved me, needed me, looked up to me. He let me get him out of his mother's house, get him a job, and move him into a cute apartment with me far from his dysfunctional family. I socialized with his friends, with whom I had nothing in common. Applauded while he sang off-key at open mics where rock stars with beer guts and outdated '80s hair relived their high school battle-of-the-bands glory days.

He cheated on me relentlessly. He humiliated me publicly by denying that I was his girlfriend. He slept with my best friend. He crashed my father's car, fled the scene of the accident, ended up in jail, let me get him a lawyer and get him free, and still, even behind bars, had other girls coming to visit him. He would tell me I didn't have to come and see him on visiting day, that I shouldn't trouble myself, then I'd find out he had his other "girlfriends" there to visit him. My mother and I scrambled to get him a lawyer and get him an appeal and get him free. He was only mildly grateful as he was having a good time in jail drawing tattoo designs for the other inmates and making pennies a day as a trustee cleaning the cells. Some people like the structure and confines of prison life. He made me feel that by getting him out I was ruining his fun. His famous line was, "I didn't ask you to do that."

He was tall, good looking, covered in tattoos, but only on the front of his body so he "could see them," a classic narcissist. My neighbors would tell me they saw girls coming into and out of my apartment all day while I was at school or work. He'd tell them tales about me being a monster. He referred to me as "that thing back at the apartment who thought I was his girlfriend." In his tales to get sympathy from people he was always the victim. No one questioned his side of the story. They all wanted to be the rescuers, the "good guys" to come and save him.

He craved new, fresh narcissistic supply at all times. No one girl would ever be enough for him. He was allergic to obligation, duty, reciprocity, or anything that would interfere with his next dose of buy-in to his false persona as a poor, misunderstood victim who just wanted to be loved. But love was never enough for him. He was bored so easily. He needed a constant supply of new admirers to keep his addiction fed.

I stayed with this abuser for four years because I was afraid I couldn't pay the bills on my own.

I've carried this hurt somewhere inside me, hidden in the folds of fat, tucked away so I wouldn't have to feel it, since 1997.

Today, I finally looked back at those four years of suffering and cried.

December 5, 2006

Better and Better

It's getting better all the time. I can walk from my car to my classroom (about 150 yards or so) without stopping for a break. I walk more and waddle less. I can put one foot in front of the other. I'm starting to care more about my appearance, buying myself clothes that fit me at this size rather than swimming in the largest size the fat store has to offer. I'm not at 100 percent wellness. I'm not even at 90 percent, but I'm approaching a better state of health.

I can walk!

Rock on.

December 8, 2006

SHOWERS AND HAMS

TODAY, I STOOD IN THE shower. Most people do, except for the elderly, the infirmed, and the physically challenged. That's why they sell shower seats in the Ronco reacher/grabber clever-gizmos catalogs, but I've been too fat even to do that. I tried the shower seat. It forced me to sit facing the tub spigot, my knees tightly together with no way to wash myself. It wasn't very sturdy. I left it at the curb in front of my parents' house.

Most people stand in the shower. I did not. It hurt too much. I was out of breath. Holding my body upright was a workout that I could not sustain. Instead, I sat on the edge of the tub with the shower curtain tucked under me to keep the shower water inside the tub. I've been showering while sitting on the tub ledge for years.

Strange that since the surgery, the shower curtain isn't keeping the water in the tub. I've been carefully tucking it underneath me, same as I've always done, yet every time I step out of the shower onto the bath mat, the floor is soaked. I have had to pile newspapers and towels on the floor to absorb the inevitable post-shower flood. They've been soaked to the point of dripping.

Before the surgery, sitting on the tub ledge was de rigueur. The floor only flooded by accident, once in a while when the shower curtain wasn't tucked in just right. Since the surgery, although I've been tucking it in just right, the water spills out onto the floor every time. I figured it was a sign. It's as if the universe was conspiring to annoy me, just enough, so that I would get tired of sopping up the flood.

Today, I was tired of it, so instead of sitting with the shower curtain tucked under me, I stood.

It reminded me of the woman who was preparing a holiday feast. She cut the ends off the ham and placed it in the large roasting pan surrounded by yams and pineapple. Her daughter, who was with her in the kitchen, asked, "Mom, why do you cut the ends off the ham that way? Does it have something to do with the flavor?"

The mother thought for a moment and answered, "Gee, I don't really know. That's the way my mother always did it. She always cut the ends off the ham. Why don't you ask her?" So the daughter approached her grandma, who was in the other room.

She asked, "Grandma, why do you always cut the ends off the ham?" Grandma answered that it was the way *her* mother had always done it.

So the young lady called her great-grandma in hopes of solving the mystery. Great Grandma answered, "When I was raising my family we were very poor. We only had one roasting pan and it was too small for the ham. In order to make it fit, I had to cut off the ends."

The shower was my ham, my roasting pan that was never big enough to accommodate the ends of the ham. I forgot to ask why I had been sitting.

I've lost enough weight so that standing isn't so much of a burden. My roasting pan is big enough now.

Today, I stood in the shower.

December 10, 2006

INCREDIBLE SHRINKING WOMAN

I'M TAKING UP LESS SPACE and becoming more noticeable. Funny how being so large meant that I disappeared from people's eyes. No, I take that back. I disappeared from my own eyes and projected a coat of armor onto myself, an outer shell to hide the inner me.

I think people see what I want them to see about me. If I'm hiding behind my body fat and begging the world not to notice me, the world will oblige. If I'm trying to be present in the world and offering myself up, flaws and all, with openness to what the world has to say for itself, about itself, about me, to me, then I'll show up for people. Less armor equals more visibility.

So, when I'm pissed off at the counter guys at the post office who are suddenly flirting and friendly, because they didn't lift me up with their approval when I thought I most needed it, it's because I'm suddenly there for them, fat as I am, accepting their energy, whereas before, I was shut down, tromped on by the enemy of self-doubt, invisible and unreceptive, so no one smiled at me.

I'm the incredible shrinking woman, showing up as I disappear.

December 11, 2006

Grabbing for Traction

The enemy is not some horned devil holding a pitchfork guarding the gates of hell. The enemy is in my head. The enemy is self-doubt, fear, and unexpressed intentions.

The enemy is on the move.

I succeeded at something, and now the enemy wants to tear me down. The back-to-back talks I gave in two mental health classes this week were well received. The students seemed engaged. They asked questions. They paid attention. A few were moved to tears. I told the story of getting the weight-loss surgery and how it's changing me. I spin an emotional tale.

After the talks, I spun on a manic high, riding the intoxication of success right into teaching my own classes the next day, but inside I still felt foolish, freakish, and ugly. I felt that I was not good enough to be in front of my own classroom. The enemy was whispering in my ear that I was too fat, too old, too saggy to deserve attention or respect. I stood in front of my students and wanted to disappear.

The fat brings me shame but it also gives me traction. It slows me down. It makes me do less than my best because of all the energy it takes to haul it around. Being fat and sick means no one expects too much from me. No one expects excellence from a middle-aged fat woman.

That's changing. I have more energy lately. I'm more alert. I'm thinking more, feeling more, doing more, and I'm scared. I'm afraid of being out of control, of doing or saying something foolish, of getting into trouble, of being vulnerable.

I have that "now or never" feeling. I'm grabbing for traction as I speed ahead into some unknown realm of higher achievement.

I hope I don't hit a wall.

December 13, 2006

Plopping Around

I'VE BEEN DRAGGING MYSELF FROM chair to chair, couch to stool, seat to bench, plopping around like a sack of potatoes with legs. I know where all the benches are on my university's campus. If you need to know where the elevators are, ask me. I've found them all. I can tell you every place there is to sit between buildings and parking lots. I've needed to rest several times when I'm walking on my way from here to there.

I've been slouching. I've been too weak to hold up my own weight. Sitting upright actually counts as exercise, but I'm changing.

They say old habits die hard and they're right. I plop around out of habit. I get up first thing in the morning and plop down on the sofa to check my blood sugar. I drag my ass to the kitchen and plop down on the strategically placed stool to wash dishes and take care of the cats. I lumber over to the computer desk and plop in the chair to check my e-mail.

Today, I noticed. I noticed that standing up and sitting upright doesn't hurt as much as it once did. The plopping is a habit, not a necessity.

I had a stack of boxes to be mailed. I needed to apply delivery confirmation stickers to each box. I was about to wheel my computer chair over to the stack when it dawned on me: I could stand next to the stack rather than sit. So, I did. I stood on my own two feet. It didn't really hurt that bad.

So, I stood at the sink to do the dishes. That didn't really hurt that bad either. As I was checking my e-mail, I sat up straight in the chair. It felt good. It felt like exercise, holding up all the heavy flesh with my poor, weak, underused muscles, but it also felt powerful.

My knee still hurts. My left leg swells if I'm on it for too long. Sometimes I still need to get the weight off of it to ease the swelling. I'm not ready to give up my kitchen stool just yet.

I know change takes time and effort. I'm willing to begin a rehab plan to strengthen my body.

Little by little, step-by-step. I'm not expecting miracles. But, then again maybe I should.

December 15, 2006

THE BURNING FLAP

MY ABS HANG DOWN TO my knees. Looking like this makes me want to curl up in an ass-ball and hide from the world. I have some nerve trying to make it in the world in this deformed state. Or is it just the enemy talking?

My abs are hanging like loose drapery. I've heard it called "the pannus." Sounds like a droopy bread basket. Maybe that's exactly what it is. It pulls on my upper carriage. The skin folds burn. I feel ugly.

I dread the work it will take to yank my body back into shape. I need to love myself stronger and harder. I need to push myself to move. I've been avoiding movement.

Moving makes me *feel* myself. My body becomes real when I feel it wiggling and jiggling around. The pannus screams for attention when I hear it flapping against my upper thighs. I feel disgusting. What if someone hears it?

I hate it. I hate that it's attached to me. I hate that I'm stuck with it till I can have it cut off.

I know how to get rid of it. It's going to take some serious work. Step one: deflate.

The more fat I lose, the less dangerous and expensive the surgery (abdominoplasty) to remove the hanging belly.

Step two: Tighten up my body.

As I deflate, increase lean body mass by moving, lifting, stretching and getting fit.

Deflating is easier because of the surgery. I simply can't eat all that much. The moving is hard. The moving means I have to FEEL my body and become acutely aware of its odd shape and melting, hanging, jiggling parts while I create a healthy musculature.

There are mirrors in every gym. I can't escape. This is such a monumental task. I'm at the foot of Mount Everest looking up.

God, help me.

December 17, 2006

SITTING AND CIRCULATION

I'M THINKING OF PUTTING OUT an exercise video called *Sitting and Circulation* for people like me, people at square one of a fitness routine, bedridden folks, the elderly, the wheelchair bound, fancy working people who don't want to work up a sweat in their nice clothes, people who are afraid of moving.

I've tried beginners' workout videos. I've tried fat-woman-in-front- of-the-room workout videos. I've tried to sweat with the oldies. The closest anyone ever came to providing a starting-from-square-one beginners' workout was Susan Powter. She taught us to modify our movements for our fitness level. Decrease range of motion. Do it in half-time. Breathe. Breathe. Breathe. But her fat-prejudiced remarks were a bit much. I felt ashamed rather than empowered.

Shame has been a tool of motivation, one that works in the short-term but never the long run. I've been yelled at by well-meaning loved ones. *Move!* Get out of your comfort zone! *Walk*, for God's sake! You're strolling, not walking! *Faster!*

Yelling and scolding scared me, but it never motivated me and I'm sure it doesn't motivate anyone else—not for long, anyway. Ignoring my ripped-up knee, forgetting my diminished lung capacity, denying my beginner fitness level, and pushing myself too hard has left me beaten and defeated. It makes me associate movement with shame and pain.

I'm not lazy. I've got gumption. Why do people yell at me like I'm lazy?

The summer before last, I was working out at the university gym four times a week at 7:00 a.m. without fail. I met a few of the gals from my peer support group, Eating and Body Image, there and we cheered each other on. I was the leader, so I was there reliably every day, even if none of the others could make it. I was the example, the rock, and I did it.

I know I can do it again, but right now I'm at square one, so I'm like Rocky in a computer chair working my way up to the gym beginning January 2, 2007.

While I'm waiting for pages to populate and images to load on my computer, I pick up my three-pound hand weights. I breathe deeply. I raise my arms above my head.

While I'm watching TV, I do leg lifts and foot twirls. I stand in the shower. I stand at the sink to do dishes. By January 2, I'll be ready for the stationary bike, the only bike I know that starts peddling at the bottom of Mount Everest.

December 18, 2006

Nothing Succeeds Like Success

HERE I AM, BLAZING THE neural pathways to success like little bulldozers in my brain. I've been addicted to misery and self-doubt for too long. My life was in the hands of the enemy. I have rescued myself. I will not be a pawn for the Prince of Darkness any longer.

Maybe blogging looks simple. Sitting and typing seems easy. It's not. Every time I sit to write in this blog I have to take an honest look at myself, my failures, shortcomings, and flaws and humbly admit that I need to work on myself. I need to haul an ice pick into the side of Everest and pull myself up over and over and over. It's daunting.

I got myself into this mess. I'm not blaming myself because blame is not powerful, it's karma-reducing. I take responsibility for myself. I chose to soothe myself with food and substances because I refused to pick my head up out of the shit-swamp of depression and see the light of hope poking through the clouds of my consciousness. Self-soothing was the best I could do.

I was weak and frightened. Afraid of my own feelings. Weak from defeat. But will is stronger than any demon. Will is the power of the divine blazing through the human spirit. Will got me up and dressed and fitted with climbing gear.

I've been talking about blogging since the surgery and yes, I did do a little of it, maybe weekly ever since August. But I longed to step it up a notch. I wanted to live more intentionally. I wanted the motivation to blog every day.

I got that motivation after taking the risk of telling my story in front of a classroom and accepting the encouragement of others. A few hugs, a few appreciative words, a hard-core recommendation to read motivational stuff, my commitment to blog without fail and—*wham*—success. Success without fail.

With each day that I keep my word, I get stronger and stronger. With each day that I sit here and face down my demons, I get tougher and tougher. With each day that I stick to my promise I believe in myself more and more.

The neural pathways in my brain get deeper and deeper and more so- lidified. A physical habit is formed.

Success becomes who I am. A climber, knowing in the depths of my being,

I will reach the summit.

December 19, 2006

Mother Complains

I was talking with my eightythree-year-old mother on the phone two days ago, and she sounded mopey.

After a lifetime of interpreting her passive aggression, I knew something was wrong, and by "wrong," I mean I must have done something to displease her. I asked her if everything was all right. I prodded and she told me she had lost interest in going out to eat and shopping. This is significant, because I am the one with whom she goes out to eat and shops. I asked if it had anything to do with me.

She answered that I only ever want to go to the local diner (whereas in the past we went to all-you-can-eat buffets) and order the steamed vegetable platter (in the past I ordered and ate God-knows-what oversized portion of something). She didn't say the things I just put in parentheses— I added them as a way to explain all this to you, my reader.

She said that I whine and make faces at my food and that it was too expensive for her to pay $25 or $30 for food that I didn't even eat or enjoy. As usual, I consoled her. I told her that I could probably find some nice nonfat options at our old all-you-can-eat-buffet haunts and that we didn't have to go to the diner any more. She perked up and we made a plan to go to a nice Pan-Asian place in Montclair this Friday. A nice restaurant, not a buffet, so that I could bring home the leftovers and she could feel like she got her money's worth.

At the time, I didn't realize how awful I felt when after we talked. How could my mother, a woman who cares for me, actually complain about the very behavior that's saving my life?

I'm disappointed. I'm angry with her. If I am going to live with the level of integrity that I know will save me, I will have to tell her that I felt hurt. I don't relish the idea. She often cries when I express myself in a self-affirming, boundary-forming way. I'll have to do it with calm and compassion, which will be hard since I am angry and disappointed. I'll have to be the bigger person, as usual, and contain my emotions like I'm talking to an overly sensitive child.

Yesterday, I was out Christmas shopping. I got myself a nice haircut. I bought myself fancy hair care products. I was in self-nurture mode. I felt the need to eat. I don't say the word "hungry" since the feeling is not exactly like hunger. It's a low-blood-sugar, low-energy kind of feeling. I took myself to the very diner where my mother and I had last eaten and where I had eaten only half my meal.

I was alone at a booth. I ordered soup, tomato juice, coffee, and the steamed vegetable platter.

I ate maybe a third of what I ordered. When I called the waitress over to ask for the check, I commented on all the food I left. She asked if I wanted to take it home. I told her no even though I hated to waste food.

She said it was OK and that she understood because food only tastes good when it's fresh.

I gave her a big tip.

December 20, 2006

Total Weight Loss:
Seventy-Three Pounds

Holy crap!

I'm not sure I could even lift something that weighed seventy-three pounds! And yet, I was carrying around that extra weight on my tiny frame for God knows how long! I'm ecstatic.

I had been avoiding the scale because I didn't want it to play mind games with me. What if it didn't show the number I wanted it to show? What if all the smaller-size clothes and the extra energy were the result of losing only forty or fifty pounds? What if . . . what if . . . what if . . .

I what-iffed myself right out of wanting to step on the scale, until today.

I went to the health center at school for a prescription renewal and I was feeling lucky, but you know and I know that luck has very little to do with this. It's been hard. The restlessness and depression of abstaining from overeating wore me down. No, I take that back. The restlessness and depression of abstaining from overeating bore me up!

When I began teaching this past semester, I was barely able to stand. My father had to walk me from the car to my classroom. With one arm I held onto my dad and groped my way along the wall with the other.

A student of mine said that took a lot of humility. A kind friend whose office I walked past told me I had fortitude.

I haven't given myself any credit. I figured I deserved all the suffering because I had done the damage to myself with my years of compulsive eating.

Yet, when I tell my story, people are kind and supportive, usually. There are always those who will tell me that I'm doomed to gain all the weight back just like some person or another they knew or that the surgery is only temporary and *blah blah blah*, but for the most part, people lift me up. I guess the humility with a dash of confidence that it takes to be able to tell my story is what it takes to be lifted up by others. So, I humbly say that I'm seventy-three pounds lighter and 100 percent committed to losing a whole lot more.

Maybe I'll get well, with a little luck and definitely with a whole lotta humility and fortitude.

To keep up with how I'm doing and for plenty of free tools for your own success, visit LisaSargese.com.

Find me on Instagram, Facebook, Twitter, and Tumblr for daily insights and inspiration so you can feel healthy and free!

December 21, 2006

I Do Solemnly Swear

I DON'T LIKE THE TERM "New Year's resolution" because of all the negative stigma attached to it. Besides, no one keeps them anyway. However, I *do* like the term "resolve" or the idea of being resolute. Affirming myself out in the world, staking an existential claim in an uncertain universe.

With that in mind, I do solemnly swear to work out six days a week beginning January 2, 2007. This week, I'll be joining a gym. Once school restarts, I'll go to the university gym.

The workout will include a minimum of thirty minutes of cardio, most likely the stationary bike, and two sets of ten reps on each machine.

I state this for the consumption of my readers, so they may hold me accountable for my promise.

Amen.

December 22, 2006
Sanit T. Clause + Me = Us

Are you him? I received a gift subscription today in the mail.

It arrived as a postcard announcing that "Sani T. Clause" had sent me a gift subscription to *Us Weekly* magazine. I figured it was my best buddy Matt. We sign our e-mails to each other with plays on words, so it was fitting. Why he would choose *Us Weekly* was beyond me, but it could have been for all the *Lost* celebrities that will surely be gracing the pages in 2007.

But he said it wasn't him. He liked the clever play on words and he suggested it could be a student of mine whom we both believe is worthy of such a play on words. So I e-mailed him and am awaiting his response.

It was the choice of *Us Weekly* that I just couldn't figure out. Why *that* publication?

I often claim that I watch too much TV. People know I love *House M.D.* and *Lost* and *Weeds* and so many other shows. Whoever sent it could have easily thought I was a celebrity-phile.

I checked with a few other friends and had no luck. As I was getting dressed to go to the post office to mail eBay packages, it dawned on me. I gasped.

"Us" as in "You + Me = Us." It was code! It must be some sort of romantic gesture.

A secret admirer? Me? I was dizzy with the thought of it. I dithered around, lovesick, and went out into the freezing day with no coat.

As I stood in line at the post office, then at the dollar store, then at the grocery store, I had butterflies in my stomach. Someone thought I was worthy of such a romantic (and expensive) gesture! But *who*?

Don't be shy. Let me know who you are.

What's the worst-case scenario? Even if I don't share the same feelings, so what? Someone cool enough to pull off a romantic stunt like this and make me so happy is definitely someone I'd want as a friend. So, it's a win-win, really.

Be brave. Tell me who you are!

December 23, 2006

Cruel to the Fat Girl

WHAT NEXT, PIZZAS DELIVERED TO my door for I. C. Weiner? An ugly cat and kittens by some Franklin Mint collectibles racket was delivered to me *with a bill* for $35.00.

At first, I thought it was a gift and that the bill was an error. When I opened the box, I dared to think that it was a gift from the Sani T. Claus *Us Weekly* subscription giver. A secret admirer, knowing I loved cats, in his angst ordered the gift for me and accidentally forgot to pay.

But then, as I was sifting through my junk mail, I found a bill for *Maxim* magazine stating that I had subscribed, and then another bill-me- later bill for another magazine subscription.

Am I the victim of a cruel prank? A disgruntled student making fun of me, accusing me of being a spinster, lesbian, cat lover?

I feel like that plain, overweight girl in the movie *Heathers* who wore a T-shirt that said "Big Fun." The cruel girls, the Heathers, wrote her a fake note supposedly from the handsome football player stating that he "liked" her. There's a scene in the film where Big Fun, holding the note, approaches the handsome athlete in the cafeteria. He and his friends are cruel. She's humiliated. The Heathers laugh at her pain.

Is this what the universe is delivering to me? The Heathers and the handsome athlete are laughing at me because I dared to think I had a secret admirer?

I feel like Big Fun. I had some nerve thinking I'd received a gift from a secret admirer. I had some nerve feeling attractive. I sifted through the junk mail and found the bill-me-later bill for *Us Weekly*. Whoever you are, I hope you had a good laugh.

December 25, 2006

CHRISTMAS MORN

I WAS UP EARLY. ALL my creatures were stirring. That fact that I was stirring was nothing less than a miracle.

Last year at this time I had just returned from the hospital with pneumonia. I was weak, pale, sick, and tired. I dragged myself to my parents' for our yearly Christmas breakfast and gift exchange. My parents had glassy eyes as they looked at me in my half-dead state. It was sad. I was sad. Hope was a glimmer of a memory in my mind. I was defeated.

But not this year. Last night, Christmas Eve, was the first in many years that I did not cry. I did not watch the *How the Grinch Stole Christmas* or *Rudolph, the Red-Nosed Reindeer* and his misfits while sobbing in melancholy solitude.

Instead, I watched *60 Minutes* featuring tales of human achievement and miraculous spirit: a blind, autistic boy who had virtuoso musical talents; a chubby champion swimmer who beat the odds to swim for her first time in the Antarctic waters near the South Pole; an elephant orphanage where abandoned babies are rehabbed back to life and reintegrated into the herd.

Today, I'm up, showered, dressed, made up, perfumed, and ready to go to my parents'.

I feel pretty good. Merry Christmas to me.

December 26, 2006

Naysayers

Naysayers be damned.

Is it just that they don't know any better? Or do they have a deep seated need to tear down other people so that they don't feel so inadequate? Nine out of ten folks had something negative to say about my surgery either before or after it was complete. Some told me that it was not going to "fix" everything for me, even though it has "fixed" a whole lot.

Some told me that they knew someone who had had the surgery, lost all the weight, and gained it all back. Some told me that it's easy to "cheat" the surgery and overconsume. Yet I'm finding that it's easy to eat well and consume exactly what my body needs.

Some told me that I would need four or five reconstructive surgeries to remove the excess skin after my weight loss, even though I saw it with my own eyes, a TV show about a woman who lost *all* her excess weight and only needed *one* surgery to remove the excess flesh from five sites on her body.

Some warned me that, because I said I couldn't wait to get my breasts redone, I would become addicted to plastic surgery and never be satis- fied with what I look like. Yet I'm reading many patients are satisfied and uplifted by their surgical uplifting and never return for more cosmetic surgery.

Oh, the friggin' list goes friggin' on.

Do they think they're trying to *help* me? Trying to prevent me from expecting too much? Warning me of the realities of the downside of things? Or maybe my high, happy, hypomanic state makes them uneasy and they're compelled to knock me down a few pegs.

I'm like Han Solo: never tell me the odds. If I want to fly into an asteroid field to lose the Imperial enemy, then I will. If I want my surgery to be a success for me, then it will.

If I know in my soul that I can make a *huge* commitment and work out six days a week because that's what a champion would do, then I will. Great things are accomplished with great vision and great risk.

I am ready.

December 28, 2006

Afraid of the Energy

Being sick and tired is rather time consuming. Being sick and tired has consumed my life for years.

I have more energy now. I have more "awake" time. More time to feel my feelings, more time to be alive.

I'm worried. I'm afraid of all this eye-opened clarity and energy. I'm looking forward to working out six days a week, because it just might tire me out and it will definitely be killing two hours a day.

Less time to get into trouble. Less time to obsess. Less time for the devil to play in the idle hands of my mind's playground.

I'm typing this with a wrapped right wrist. I played *Bookworm* (a Scrabble-like computer game) so vigorously and for so long, I strained my wrist. I've been online quite a bit, clicking my mouse, working on eBay. I grossed over $1500 this month in eBay sales. *Clickity click. Ouch* goes the wrist.

I'm obsessive. Extreme. When I do something, I'm focused, driven, unshakable, single-minded.

That's not always healthy. If I focus on the "wrong" thing, some romantic interest for instance, the obsession can be destructive.

The upside, and there always is one, is that the extremes can lead to great accomplishments. Multiple degrees, incredible projects, beating the odds, superhuman feats. When I lose interest in an idea, after it's lost its glitter, I'm tempted to abandon it. It is usually complete before it's abandoned. I'm pretty good about finishing what I start. I start on a high then ride the momentum through the slumps.

I never leave in the middle of a degree or program or project, even if I've lost interest. I stick with it, painfully, till I've fulfilled my obligation, then it's over. This recent degree was like that. I lost interest in it during the past few semesters, but I didn't quit. I kept at it, and now it's time to buy another frame for my wall. I trust myself to complete things. Character is built by keeping one's word even when one does not feel like it.

I'm not afraid of that. I'm not afraid that I'll quit on myself. I'm afraid of the mania that comes with energy. I'm afraid I'll get into trouble, that I'll pick the wrong person, thing, idea to obsess over to use up the extra energy. This new energy is a high and highs scare me.

I'm telling myself that the gym will help me with that. It will help me focus. It will keep me even. It will use my energy wisely.

My superpowers for good.

December 31, 2006

THE FEAR

IT'S BEEN STOPPING ME FOR years: the fear. The dread.

What if I *do* lose all the weight, have a hot body, self-confidence, money, a great career, a fabulous home, a sweetheart of a boyfriend, and I'm still not happy? What if I accomplish everything I set out to do and end up with the same gaping abyss of meaninglessness that I've carried with me for all my fat years? What if all this change and transformational improvement isn't the magic bullet of bliss that I hope it will be?

Ah, screw it. I'm doing it anyway.

If I'm empty at the end of the road, I'll pick a new road and figure it out then. I know the definition of courage. It's *not* the absence of fear, it's being afraid and doing it anyway.

Happy New Year to the fearful intrepid in all of us. Blessed be.

January 1, 2007

BIG BAD GLACIER

I WAS AT A FABULOUS New Year's Eve cocktail party last night. Great food (that I couldn't eat), lovely home, interesting people, fireworks, wine, and great conversation. I was having a wonderful time. Until someone took my picture.

I was standing with a pretty woman who couldn't weigh more than 120 with her lunch and pearls. It was one of those digital cameras that shows you the picture immediately. There I was, a big mass looming in front of this slender blonde, her diamond ring gleaming and beaming her married status to the world. I felt like a giant glacier, an icy mass, huge and hulking, carving rivulets and canyons in my path. And just when I had been feeling so good about myself.

People had been giving me compliments, noticing my weight loss, telling me I looked great. Now, muffled echoes falling on deaf ears, unable to penetrate the glacier. I don't like being so big.

Now, from a feminist perspective, I should examine why I'm uncomfortable taking up space—why, as a woman, I'm so appalled at my size, my extension into the world. As an educator and counselor, I should find a way to lovingly embrace my largeness for the sake of my future clients who will need to be taught how to love themselves as they are before they try to create healthy change. I know that hating the way I look is unbalanced, unhealthy, and uncalled for.

But it's the truth. It's the truth about how I feel. The upside, and there's always an upside, is that it motivates me to want to get better, healthier, fitter, smaller.

The downside is that I may be doing the right thing for the wrong reasons. I don't want to hate myself. I don't want to punish my body. I don't want to change because I believe I'm defective. I shouldn't want to take up less space. I deserve to take up space, right?

I want to love myself exactly as I am, in the present, immensity and all. I want to honor my body and its need to be oxygenated, strong, and fit. I want to change because I see possibility, because I'm good now and can be better in the future.

Starting at the gym tomorrow will entail more than biking and lifting. It's a journey of my mind and soul as well. I have an idea that could help. I have a Sony Walkman and a Sony Discman. (Why they're not Walk- women and Discwomen is beyond me, but I digress.) While I'm on the stationary bike, pedaling steadily, inducing a hypnotic state, I'm going to listen to motivational, inspirational, and instructional materials.

Let some positive thinking penetrate my brain. Block out the critical thoughts and replace them with uplifting ones. Change my body, change my mind, change my life.

I hope it works.

January 2, 2007

CRAVING THE DISCIPLINE

I'VE RESISTED WHAT I MOST need: discipline. I've been soothing myself with indulgence for years, letting myself get away with doing what I felt like in the moment under the guise of self-care. It ended up resulting in self-defeat. My health was destroyed by my self-soothing.

I'm not going to beat myself up over this. My instincts were good. I was doing what I had to do to self-soothe. Depression is a nasty ailment. Sadness is the most painful emotion. Physical pain wears a person down, especially when it's chronic.

It's only human of me to want to feel better. Lacking a better system, I went with what worked.

In the moments of despair, pain, grief, and isolation, eating and taking it easy made me feel better.

This is why certain people won't move or exercise. It hurts! Not in the good way. Not in the "make it burn" way that brings oxygen to atrophied muscles. In the "Oh my God, I'm pushing myself too hard in an unhealthy way and ripping the shreds out of my weak, tired, sick muscles that are gasping for hydration and oxygen" way.

I watched a marathon of *The Biggest Loser* yesterday, a show I resisted watching because of the harshness and inhumane treatment of fat people. One woman claimed she was there because she had gained weight and her husband said he wasn't attracted to her anymore. Dammit, girl!

Divorce him! A loving husband would be concerned for her, but never hurt her feelings that way. I take these things personally. In the past, I rebelled by refusing to enter the exercise fray, by refusing to diet, by resisting discipline. I can't be the only one who does this, can I?

Also, the rigor of the workouts seems dangerously beyond these people's ability. A heart shouldn't go from being sedentary to pumping like an Olympic marathon runner's in such a short time when a person isn't used to it. Again, my instinct is to be resistant and rebellious. I can't be alone in this resistance and rebellion. Other people feel this, right?

Today, I begin my first day of my workout commitment at Tone Fitness in Bloomfield, New Jersey. Part of my motivation will be to get fit enough to be an inspiration to the infirmed, disabled, and depressed, to be strong enough to lift them up out of their sadness and malaise.

Discipline can be good. Discipline can build character. Doing what I don't feel like doing can make me a better person. By looking at the long- term result rather than the momentary desire, I can self-soothe with discipline. I can make myself feel less sad, less weak, stronger, able, winning!

By doing this I am *not* conspiring with a cruel, unfeeling enemy like the trainers on *The Biggest Loser*. I am not complicit with the personal trainer who says harsh things to their clients. I am not the wife who punishes her sacred flesh because of a Jack-a-lope husband. I am not the girl who hates to move. I'm doing this for me, on my terms. I am the warrior for self-care and compassion. Long live unconditional, positive regard for self and others!

I better start by learning to love what I see in the mirror. I must break the habit of fat-bashing myself.

January 3, 2007

LOVING THE FLAPPY VEAL ARMS

Yesterday was my first day of my six-days-a-week workout commitment. It went well, physically.

I did not pant or gasp for air, no severe aches or pains, reached my target heart rate easily, sustained thirty minutes of cardio, did six machines, and three pounds on the free weights. I had a bottle of water with me and drank regularly.

Knowing that the rhythmic pedaling on the stationary bike would put me in a semi-hypnotic trance, I listened to a Deepak and Dyer tape rather than let the careless lyrics of some pop song waft into my consciousness from the gym's speakers. I listened and laughed, enjoying the teaching. The thirty minutes passed quickly.

All was right with the world, until I saw myself in the mirror.

The first mirror-look happened in the bathroom. Tone Fitness is a spotless gym and their bathroom is no exception. It is spotless right down to the wall mirror, which is right across from the toilet. This is where I caught a glimpse of myself sitting on the throne with my sweatpants down around my knees. I looked like a blob of spotted ham fat.

Every blemish, every scar, showed up crimson in stark contrast to my pale skin. I hated the rolls and folds of my flesh that looked like loose dough as I moved. Stop! "Forgive, forgive, forgive," I told myself. "You're doing something about it, Lisa. Don't be so critical. Give yourself credit for wanting to change for the better. This is only temporary. Console, console, console." Part of me felt it was wrong to think so harshly of my body, but the shame and blame won out.

The consoling part of my brain worked until I climbed on the bike. As Deepak and Wayne spoke, I would catch a look at myself in the mirrored wall next to the bike. My sides were bulbous, my flanks enormous. I hated what I saw. Thankfully, the soothing voices of the two audio books helped me get off of the negative tirade in my mind.

All good until it was time for the free weights, and again, I faced a wall of mirrors. It's a tiny gym. The mirrored walls create the illusion of space. I get that. I also got that my upper arms are flappy like crated veal. I lifted and flapped, stretched and jiggled, hating the way I looked and barely acknowledging how good I felt.

I'm worried about how harshly I blame and shame myself. On an intellectual level I know that these judgmental thoughts are self-defeating and cruel. I know that in the grand scheme of reality the love and spirit that permeates every particle of the universe supports me unconditionally. It's my ego that's out of whack.

From a spiritual perspective, everyone's ego is out of whack, deluding us into believing we are separate, isolated, material, finite beings. It's ego that believes we are less worthy of love based on shallow perceptions of how our bodies rate in the current social climate. Again, on an intellectual level, I know all this.

Knowing the truth isn't enough to stop me from calling myself ugly names, hating the shape of my flesh and thinking myself unworthy of the love and respect of others. This same judgmental name-calling keeps too many people in a state of depression. The uglification of what isn't red carpet–acceptable keeps people from living to their fullest. Women, obese women like me, are especially vulnerable.

The world suffers when its inhabitants are living under a cloud of gloom and self-imposed limits. How can depression be overcome by a society full of self-defeated, spiritually sick people who have no self-esteem? Who feel they can't measure up, so they don't bother? I'll have to start with me. If I can cure myself of this mental anguish and emerge victorious, then I can help others to cure themselves. Make the world a better place. Diminish suffering. It's plan!

Tomorrow, when I look in the mirror at the gym, I am going to tell myself nice things about my flappy veal arms, starting with *not calling them flappy veal arms.*

Yesterday's weight: 308 pounds

Weights on the machines: 25–30 pounds Free weights: 3 pounds

January 5, 2007

THE GUT IN THE MIRROR

THE GYM IS A TERRIBLE place to notice a gut. I looked in the mirror as I
was working on one of the weight machines. I freaked. Seeping out from
under my pretty pink T-shirt was a doughy blob with an ass-like cleft. It
drooped half way down my thighs. My lower abs were hanging like pizza
dough, pulled toward the floor by gravity like a sack of batter.

I had no idea it was so bad. My lower abs smiled at me like a giant
clown with a cleft chin.

I dressed in a way that I thought would make it disappear, camouflaged
by long T-shirts and blouses, tucked away like a giant flabby secret inside
my pants. I was in denial about my stealth apron.

I had no idea it was visible till I saw it in the gym mirror. I had no
idea that my misshapenness was visible to the whole world. I had no idea
my body was seeping out from under my blouse like an enormous water
balloon, swinging and dangling, making me feel like a circus sideshow.

I made the mistake of telling this to my mother, hoping for consolation,
encouragement, the unconditional love a mother is supposed to give. I
told her I felt discouraged because I saw my lower blob in a way I hadn't
before. I told her how ugly I thought it was. Her answer?

"Well, Lis, it's been ugly for how long? You can't expect it to change
overnight."

Wow. She confirmed it. I was right. It *is* ugly. I'm carrying around a
giant blob of ugly hanging dangerously close to my knees. Am I supposed

to try to tell myself something different about the ugly? Try to love my giant, alien dough sack?

The upside of my mother's awful comment, and there's always an upside if you look hard enough, is that I shouldn't expect changes too quickly. This is a journey, a process, a transformation over time. Instant changes will not bring about the lasting transformation I want, and besides, instant success is just not possible unless I learn to measure it in much smaller increments. I certainly shouldn't expect a hundred pounds of fat to disappear overnight.

In the meantime, what can I do about the ugly? I've heard the expression "only a mother could love" but Mother just made me feel uglier. Now what? What if, rather than going to my mother for something she might not give, I become the mother of myself? What if I'm the one who needs to love, honor, and cherish the ugly? Mother myself. I've had to be a mother to my mother for so many years—now I have to mother myself.

I looked within, searching restlessly for something lovable, knowing there had to be one. Then it dawned on me: greatness.

What is greatness? It's the overcoming of grand obstacles, beating the odds, succeeding against adversity, prevailing when quitting would be easier, climbing Everest. This journey of transformation would be meaingless without something to transform. In order to be inspiring, I need to have a problem to overcome so my story will have meaning.

The doughy abs and what I do about them are what make my story great. Getting rid of the sack of batter *will* take time, *will* take will, *will* require courage and tenacity. Without this giant obstacle to my health and self-esteem, what would I overcome? I'd have no story if I didn't have a problem.

What good is the brave knight without the dragon? If the knight could just walk into the tower and grab the princess with no dragon to fight, what kind of story would that make? What kind of quest would that be? My flab is what makes me great.

I thank God for my flabby abs. My dragon to be slain. Yesterday's weight: 304 pounds

January 6, 2007

The Big One

Fresh from a workout at the gym, I strolled through the "big" Shop Rite, proud that I didn't opt for the smaller Stop and Shop around the corner from my apartment. I usually do opt for the Stop and Shop, because it's smaller and walking through it is easier on my joints. Yeah, I'm in a lot of pain—not from working out, just from arthritis and inflammation.

It's mostly my knee, the left one. The meniscus is torn, I think. If I'm on it for more than five minutes, it swells, stiffens, and hurts bad. I avoid situations that involve standing or walking for any length of time. Shop- ping is fun only for a few minutes, grocery shopping even less so.

For the past four days, I've been feeling great after my workouts. The warmth of increased blood flow to the knee area gives me some mobility. I've been to the "big" Shop Rite three days in a row. My cupboards and fridge are stocked with delicious, healthy foods, but it hasn't been all sunshine and roses. Yesterday, as I was walking down the aisle, I was overcome with fatigue. I suddenly felt like I didn't want to shop. Instead of feeling chipper and empowered as I had for the past few days, I felt like sitting down. I wished I had gone to the smaller Stop and Shop. I wished I didn't have to walk the length of the Shop Rite to reach the dairy aisle. I wanted to go home.

My initial reaction was to blame my character. I felt like I was lazy. I felt as if I should have more enthusiasm. I felt like it had to be something about my thinking that was wrong.

I stopped myself. I noticed what I was feeling. It was my knee. It hurt bad. It throbbed and stiffened. It wasn't my character. It was my body. It makes good sense for a body to want to rest when it's injured. It makes sense to want to avoid pain. Our bodies are programmed that way. Pain signals that something is wrong. Our instincts to avoid pain are there to help keep us alive. They tell us when we're injured. They draw attention to something that requires attending.

This is why many fat people like me don't like to move. This is why those "beginners'" workouts don't work for many obese people. They hurt. They hurt, but not in a good way.

When a person feels like they have a small truck parked on their chest and it hurts to breathe, people will avoid deep breathing. When a person feels pins and needles in their joints and it hurts to stand, they'll avoid standing. Beginning a movement program from square one means something different to different people. Most beginners' workouts are way beyond square one.

For me, standing is a challenge. It works many of my muscle groups and requires deep breathing. Yeah, I said it. Standing makes me out of breath. Before the surgery, even sitting upright was a challenge. Getting up off the couch to go to the bathroom was a workout (still is some nights). I can't be alone in this. Sweatin' to the oldies seems like a far distant goal, an advanced program for a future me. This isn't "stinkin' thinkin'," either. This is my own common sense based on my fitness level. Getting out of my comfort zone shouldn't have to mean hopping around on my bad knee trying to keep up with an aerobics routine that I'm not ready for.

Out of shape folks need to start smart. Work our way up to the so called "beginners'" programs.

We must do this lovingly, with great praise for ourselves and without any harsh taskmasters trying to tell us how much or how fast we should move.

I remember a student who was a fitness major, a self-appointed motivational coach who happened to be leading a cardio class, wagging her finger at me and yelling, "You're not walking, you're strolling! *Move!*" Weighing close to four hundred pounds, my strolling felt like marathon running. I was in pain. I was out of breath. I resented her for talking down to me. I was doing the best I could.

My reaction? Rebel. Never go to class again. Avoid moving.

Now I'll avoid moving unless I can do it alone with no one scolding me, but how nice it would be to have someone telling me that I'm good, brave, worthy, and doing a wonderful job. A wise person once taught me not to look at what's wrong with a thing, but to find what's missing and then contribute that missing element.

I didn't have a cheering section when I sat up on the couch and took deep breaths.

No one applauded me when I sat upright at the computer and sucked in my stomach, tucked in my butt and kept my shoulders down. The only feedback I got was the rush of blood bringing oxygen to the neglected parts of my body. Thankfully, it was enough. It kept me wanting more.

Moving in a smart way feels good. Life wants life.

I can say nice things to myself in my head, replace the harsh taskmaster that yaps automatically whenever I feel weak. I can blog and encourage others for taking small steps. When one of you comments with a "way to go," believe me, I glow.

Yesterday's weight: 306 pounds

Today is day five of my six-days-a-week workout commitment. I think I hear you cheering.

January 10, 2007

Toilet versus Life

LIFE IS WINNING. IT'S BEATING the bathroom. There was a time, recently, and for a long-ass time, that taking my morning crap was more fun than the rest of my day.

It's understandable. It feels good. It's a sitting activity, no joint pain, no heavy breathing, no pressure. I get to read magazines. My cats wander in and out of the bathroom (I live alone so I keep the bathroom door open), enjoying their various rituals. Leo will jump up on the sink and demand a thin stream of water from the tap. Sebastian comes in and warbles pathetically or jumps up in my arms while I'm on the throne till I pet all twenty pounds of him. Gabriel gets up on his enormous hind legs and extends his paw up into my face to announce that he's waiting for breakfast. Jacob will sit outside the bathroom and watch me impatiently. The baby, Bosie, jumps inside my pants that are down around my ankles and attacks the other cats through the fabric.

It's quite a party.

Often I will sit there, long after my business is complete, just enjoying the no-pressure me-time. No computer, no e-mails to read, no phone to answer, no chores that have to be done at that moment, no urgency to exercise or shop or cook or clean.

Today, I was impatient as I pooped. I wanted to get it over with. I had no desire to linger. I flipped through *US Magazine*, my gift from the mysterious Sani T. Claus, looked at the gaunt celebrities, admired their lives, and felt anxious to get on with mine. I wanted to get my pills, insulin, and coffee in me so I could shower and get to the gym.

This is a big change. When I first started my workouts, I thought I would dread going to the gym. I thought I would have to fight with myself and convince myself to go. I expected it to suck. It doesn't. I actually like it.

Working out is a long, extended, me-time frolic. No phones, no computers, no chores, no pressure—just me and my machines. Triumph. Satisfaction. One step closer to wellness.

The mirrors still bug me, but not as much. I *do* see changes in the mirror. My triangle-shaped upper arms are slightly smaller. My flanks don't seem so daunting now that I know in my heart that they're shrinking. I can look myself in the eye and feel good about the girl looking back at me. She's taking care of me and I'm taking care of her. We're starting to love each other.

January 10, 2007
I KEEP MY WORD

I WAS UP AT 5:45 a.m. today because I have to be at school at 9:00 a.m. I'm sitting here with my coffee and my (homemade) tamari almonds, keeping my word. If I don't keep my word, the guilt will hang like an albatross around my neck and weigh me down till I fall down . . . dead.

Maybe I'm supposed to think that keeping my word makes me a champion. I kinda think that way. More so, I think that *not* keeping my word makes me a loser.

I don't *have* to blog every day. I don't *have* to go to the gym six days a week. I *said* I would blog every day. I *said* I would go to the gym six days a week. I guess I *choose* to keep my word.

All day, I'll be up at school for a day of diversity training beginning at 9:00 a.m. The workshops should end around 4:30 p.m. I know I'll be tired by the end of the day. There's no way I want to push myself to go to the gym in that condition. The best way for this to work would be to work out in the morning before I have to be ready for the 9:00 a.m. meetings.

It would be easier for me to just skip the gym today and maybe work out on Sunday to make up the time. It would have been easier to stay in bed when the alarm went off this morning.

It would be easier to sit here and find a good excuse to work online till it's time to shower rather than go out in the cold and drive to the gym. Thing is, I've taken the easy route too many times and ended up hating myself. I could lie and say that my goal of wellness and fitness and beauty are what got me up and out of the bed today. Maybe it would sound more like champion speak. But I won't lie.

What got me up out of the bed today was knowing how *shitty* I would feel if I stayed in bed and skipped my workout. It would put a black stain on the clear slate of integrity and trust I'm building with myself. When I give my word, I mean it. When I promise myself something, I don't take the easy road and let myself off the hook because "I don't feel like it" or some such lame excuse. Breaking my word wears away at my self-respect.

Some might call this being hard on myself. I would disagree. I've been hard on myself.

I've called myself negative names like "fat," "lazy," and "ugly." I've neglected my nutritional needs and fed myself drive-thru junk because it was easy and I was too tired to feed myself better foods. I've broken my word to myself in the name of taking it easy.

I won't make excuses today. I'm going to the gym. I'm blogging. I'm doing this because I want to keep my word. I want to keep my integrity. My desire to be the genuine article strikes again.

Having kept my word, I can enjoy my day-long workshop with no guilt and nothing to dread. At the end of the day when I'm tired, I can rest with a clear conscience.

That's being kind to myself, a commitment of champions.

January 11, 2007

CREATIVITY KILLS PAIN

I WAS STANDING IN THE shower. If you remember, from a previous post, standing in the shower is a big deal for me. This is new behavior since I've been washing myself whilst sitting on the tub ledge for years. Standing was exhausting.

Standing is still a challenge. Sometimes my legs hurt. Sometimes I'm out of breath. Sometimes I'm just tired and don't feel like standing; but, I haven't sat. I've toughed it out, not to be hard on myself, but to feel alive, to experience what's possible, to push a little harder for continued wellness.

I was in the shower, tired, a bit winded, having just eaten. I leaned against the wall. I wanted to sit. I argued with myself inside my head for a bit, won my own argument, and remained standing. I chose to tough it out. Having made the decision, my head moved onto a new subject as I washed myself with a variety of scented soaps and crèmes, a different one for each part of my body, delightful self-pampering. My mind moved onto an upcoming peace conference at my university and the proposal I planned to write in order to speak at the event. Potential titles and topics flitted through my brain. I began to create different phrases and conceptual anchors for my speech.

Then I noticed something as the hot water was beating down on me. It was no longer difficult to stand in the shower. Nothing hurt. Breathing was easy. I felt great. It was as if the flurry of creativity in my mind had magically erased my discomfort or the pain was no longer so great that it dominated my thinking. With less pain, I now have new space in my mind to fill with other things. How will I get used to this?

January 12, 2007
HAPPY YET?

I'M TIRED OF POSTPONING MY own happiness until some future time. Can't I be happy now?

Can't I be happy with exactly who I am? I've been seduced by the idea that I'll be happy, entitled to happiness, deserving of love, appealing, interesting, and worthy only when I've achieved some distant body weight. Is it even possible to be happy in the now?

God bless Susan Powter. Back in the mid-1990s, she helped me. I bought her *Stop the Insanity* package that included a workout tape, audio tape, books, and assorted goodies. On her workout tape, she introduced the idea of modification. That is, when you're working out to a video routine or in a class, you must modify the moves to fit your fitness level. You don't have to do it exactly as the instructor tells you. People at square one should move in half the time, half the motion, smaller moves, and so on. She didn't expect everyone in the class to work out at her pace. It was refreshing. I followed Susan at my own modified pace. I felt validated.

On her audio tape she gave her listeners permission to eat. She stressed the need to eat, breathe, and move in order to reduce body fat. When I first heard her say that it was OK to eat, I cried. I was so relieved. My miserable, growling furnace of a stomach didn't feel like such an unreasonable demon. It was hungry. Feeding it was good. It's what humans do. Powter preached that eating whole foods, high-fiber foods, and low-fat foods was more filling and nutritious, leading to fewer cravings. She stressed that we should eat when we're hungry and eat till we're full—just make it carrots rather than corn chips.

I worshipped her. She was re-mothering me with her words, giving me permission to nourish myself. Even though she was clear about fat being the enemy (which made me feel like my body was the enemy) and leaned toward veganism, I still felt an expansive permission from her to put food in my mouth without guilt.

Using her methods, I lost over thirty pounds. Why I gained it back plus some is a topic for another blog, if not a book! I think being on such a low-fat diet was not really healthy for me. I still believe in some of her methods and use them as they suit my needs.

Problem was, she talked about fatness like it was something horrible. Though I love her outspokenness, I never really forgave her for what she said about obese women. I don't remember if it was on a tape or in an interview, but she was commenting on a photography exhibit featuring the naked bodies of obese women. Her comment went something like this, "How can you look at all that ugly fat and call it beautiful?"

I was wounded. How could she be so harsh? She had seemed so encouraging and accepting. Now she was fat-bashing! I felt like she was telling me to hate my body, my self, my image. Was she calling me ugly? I internalized her opinion, and the anti-fat opinions of society in general. If I was fat, I was ugly. If I had fat on my body, it needed to be removed by any means necessary.

I went through years of fat-acceptance reading. I looked in the mirror and called myself beautiful. I looked at statues of goddesses who had bodies like me. I went online and joined fat-positive discussion boards. I placed ads on BBW dating sites. I instant messaged with BBW lovers. I tried so hard to convince myself that I was beautiful just the way I was. It worked for a while, but my inflated self-esteem didn't last. The depression, illness, and pain changed my mind. I blamed my fat for my feelings.

Here I am in the present, looking in the mirror and hating my fat. Is this right? Was Powter correct in her assessment that fat is ugly?

Compared to our society's red-carpet ideal, I suppose it is. But in the art world, what society finds ugly can be beautiful and meaningful. Shapes are just shapes. I think fat is value-neutral. We impose value on it. Fat is fat . . . and then we have our stories about it.

Susan Powter's story and her label of "ugly" was based on her own experience of reaching her own optimum health. When she was overweight, she was depressed, sedentary, and unhealthy. For her, fat represented all those unpleasant memories. Seeing fat on others triggered those negative feelings for her and served as justification for her comment on how ugly those fat women were in the photographs. Her comments were more of a reflection of her feelings about herself. Too bad she felt the need to project onto those of us who are trying to be fat, fit, and in love with our bodies as they are.

When I look in the mirror and see my upside down Valentine ab apron, I see hurt and rejection and pain. I see a swinging glob of way-too- heavy-lard that knocks things over on my coffee table when I scoot by on my way in and out of the room. I see my own body as evidence that I've neglected myself in favor of denial and overeating. I see near-lethal levels of blood sugar. A deadly staph infection. Joint pain. Cruel comments from family and peers. Fat prejudice. Bullying. Ill-fitting clothes. Back pain. Grotesque obesity that separates me from others. Guys who don't ask me out. It must be that I'm ugly.

She's still at it. I found Susan Powter's website. She's still calling fatness an ugly health hazard. I don't find that encouraging at all. I wrote her off. I sold my Powter stuff on eBay.

I felt betrayed. She was no longer on my side.

I do want to be strong and healthy. I want to be happy. Do I have to be lean to make that happen? Do I have to be fatless to be worthy of happiness?

January 14, 2007

FAT LOVE

DEEPAK CHOPRA SAYS WE HUMANS go around looking for love the way a fish swims around looking for water. We're surrounded by it and blind to it at the same time.

I haven't had a boyfriend in years. It hurts when I think of that. Of course, I blame my size.

Online, there's plenty of proof that fat women get boyfriends. I see wedding pictures of fat women getting married. I ask overweight friends if they were heavy when they met their boyfriends/husbands/lovers, and they say, "Yes." I see fat couples out in public. I see fat people paired up with thin people.

So, what's my problem?

Maybe it's not the men. Maybe it's me. Maybe my erroneous belief that I'm unlovable because I'm fat keeps me isolated. Maybe it's my wobbly attempts at self-love that keep men at a distance. I always heard that you have to love yourself first before anyone else can love you. But, do these women who *do* have partners necessarily have all their shit together? Don't I deserve to have some love and affection *while* I'm fighting so hard to get all my sh*t together?

I really don't know.

January 17, 2007

Some Gorgeous Guy

I WAS STUNNED. I WAS at the gym using one of the leg extension machines looking straight ahead as I always do, not wearing the headphones, just minding my own business, talking to myself in my head. The front door opened and cold air blasted briefly into the room.

Someone spoke. It was a male voice. The guy on the upright bike, just inches from me, had said something in my direction. I looked over at him expecting to discover that he had been addressing someone else or that he was telling me I had dropped or broken something.

He was gorgeous. He looked like the actor Ivan Sergei. He glistened with sweat. I made some sort of noise signaling that I hadn't heard him. "It doesn't feel so great. The cold," he said, speaking a bit more loudly and trying to enunciate. I mumbled something incomprehensible about a cold blast and nodded sympathetically. He smiled.

I turned to look straight ahead as if he wasn't there. I've been anonymous for so long, protected by an invisible shield of my presumed unworthiness, I had no idea how to react. Cute guys don't make friendly comments to me. At least, they haven't in twenty years or so.

I've been content to not exist, hidden by my socially unacceptable fat. I've become accustomed to the isolation, the anonymity. If I couldn't be accepted, I would simply fade into the background, disappear like a nonperson. His friendly comment threw me. I was new to me.

I had no idea people could even see me.

January 19, 2007

Hunger Pangs

Yesterday, I experienced my first hunger pangs since the gastric bypass surgery. That means I've gone almost six months without feeling hungry. I awoke from a deep nap. I hadn't eaten in five hours or so. The hunger actually propelled me out of bed!

The hunger disturbed me. I haven't felt this kind of hunger since August. I thought actual hunger pangs were a thing of the past. How could this tiny little pouch of a stomach feel hungry?

I'm consoling myself with the notion that my workouts are making me hungry, that hunger is normal, that my body needs the fuel to function. Looking back on what I'm eating in a day, I really have no reason to panic. Breakfast is a slice of protein bread with nonfat cheese and some ketchup, with a stein of coffee sweetened with Equal and lightened with fat-free half-and-half. Lunch is usually sushi rolls. Snacks include fresh peppers, celery, apples, sugar-free Jell-O, low-fat yogurt, edamame, fat-free pretzels or sugar-free ice pops. Dinner might be fat-free turkey, tuna tartar, egg beaters, sushi rolls. I feel like I'm a "clean" eater.

Yet, the hunger pisses me off. I went through all this surgical suffering so I'd never have to feel hungry again. I don't like feeding my furnace. I don't like the feeling of emptiness in my gut. I don't like the demanding behavior of my stomach. I hate my stomach as if it's an alien to me, not part of me, not on my team. My stomach feels like the enemy.

Intellectually, I know that my stomach is not plotting against me. My stomach is a part of me, part of the team, part of the whole person. When my body needs fuel, it's my stomach's job to bang around a bit and get my attention. So, where does my animosity come from?

I think my stomach has taken the rap for my eating disorder. I've blamed my stomach for the emptiness in my heart, the abyss caused by my need to feel nurtured. The gut that once processed food as if it were a bottomless pit—never filled, never satisfied, always wanting more—was the scapegoat for my neglected inner child, the child who wanted me to love her and care for her, who craved encouragement and cherishing, who seemed as if she'd never be satisfied, no matter how much I loved her. When I get hungry, I'm reminded of my neediness. Having needs is dangerous. They might not be filled. I might be shamed for them. That's what I learned in childhood.

My stomach ended up as the stand-in for my sad, inner child whom I hated for being weak and needy. I hate her because she puts me in the position of being rejected, neglected, starved.

If I take care of her and love her, maybe she won't growl so much like she's ready to attack. Maybe if I feed her gently and lovingly, she'll calm down and coexist with the rest of me cooperatively and peacefully.

January 20, 2007
MY BEAUTY HANG-UP

I'VE BEEN READING FASHION MAGAZINES since I was eleven years old, coincidentally the same age my menses began. There must be some connection between my self-image, my womanhood, and the effects of glamour culture.

In the past, I've beaten myself up for loving celebrities and their red-carpet parading. There was a time that I believed I should forsake pop culture in order to heal my self-esteem. I believed that indulging my fascination with supermodels and celebrities was somehow selling out my gender, that my love of the Hollywood glitterati was making an indelible impression of a narrow beauty ideal on my fragile psyche.

During my fat-positive quest when I weighed around four hundred pounds, I devoured positive depictions of big women, fabulous fat artwork, Rubens, *Radiance* magazine, Emme, pre-op Carnie Wilson, pre-op Ann Wilson, pre–Jenny Craig Kirstie Alley, pre–Trim Spa Anna Nicole Smith, Roseanne, Taurus Vixen, Mo'Nique, and many other plus-size beauties. It worked. I convinced myself that I was beautiful just the way I was. That's a good thing, and I encourage people of all sizes and shapes to do whatever it takes to build self-esteem and acknowledge inner and outer beauty in all its divine manifestations.

I ceased to be self-conscious when I led discussions, lectured, went out in public, and so on. When I was attracted to someone, I approached them with confidence that I was a gorgeous creature who deserved their love and attention. (They did *not* respond positively, any of them.)

I bought beautiful, sparkly clothes and jangling jewelry, bright red lipstick and luscious perfume.

I thought I was the sh*t . . . until I almost died, twice.

Instead of boosting my self-esteem and regarding myself as a goddess to be cared for, first and foremost by me, I sugarcoated my self-image, frosting it in a thick layer of denial about the state of my health. It was business as usual in all my sparkly, sweet-smelling glory: binge eating, no exercise, neglecting my out-of-control blood sugar, smoking too much, avoiding the mirror, sleeping and napping with undiagnosed sleep apnea, picking at my skin, and other self-destructive habits. I was a mess.

The first time I met Mr. Death was on my fortieth birthday. The Jack-a-lope du jour had ruined my party by not showing up. My friend Marni was scratching my back consolingly when she came across a strange lump. Nutshell version of this story is that I had multiple boils and car- buncles all over my body from a resistant staph infection exacerbated by out-of-control blood sugar. It took three weeks in an isolated room in the hospital with round-the-clock intravenous antibiotics (running around $2000 a bag, no lie) to save me.

The second time Mr. Death came to the door of my soul was with a bad case of pneumonia. Not being able to breathe is one of the scariest feelings. The upside, and there always is one, is that the pneumonia led me to follow a doctor's suggestion to be tested for sleep apnea. I tested *severe*, only breathing 60 percent of my sleeping time. That's scary. Now, sleeping with a continuous positive airway pressure (CPAP) machine for the past year has saved me from a likely stroke or heart attack.

Look, I'm not saying that *every* obese person is at death's door. Yes, we do suffer discrimination from every aspect of society, especially the medical community, but I'm not afraid to say that I was in denial when I used positive fat imagery to mask much deeper and dangerous health issues. I was fat and beautiful on the outside but I ignored how sick I was on the inside.

I'm torn between wanting to feel good in the body I have and wanting to experience the privilege and ease of being smaller. I think of the prayer that I saw on a T-shirt once that said, "God, please let me hit the lottery so I can prove to you that money won't ruin me!" God, please let me be slender, fit, and healthy so I can prove to you that I won't let all the atten- tion ruin my character.

Let me walk that red carpet in a designer gown with my arms and back and neck showing. I promise not to be shallow. I promise not to let it ruin me. I promise not to believe that happiness fits in a ball gown or that changing my body will fix all my problems, but please let me feel that confidence just once. You can turn me back into a pumpkin at midnight if you have to.

January 22, 2007

Sleep Guilt and Garbage Surfing

I SLEPT IN TODAY. NOT just till 9:00 a.m. or 10:00 a.m. but till 2:00 p.m.! It wasn't one of those "roll over and look at the clock," "tossing and turning," "dreading the day" kind of sleeps. It was a "get up at 7:00 a.m. to pee then dirt nap till two o'frickin' p.m. in the afternoon" sleep.

I forgot what finally awakened me. Was it one of the cats impatient for his brunch? Was it the end of a disturbing dream about not finding the route home on a road trip gone bad?

Or did I simply need the sleep until I didn't?

At first, I looked at the clock and panicked. How could I have slept away the morning? My mornings are precious to me. I love my disciplined, daily activities. Reading something uplifting on the pooper, making fra- grant coffee, reading and answering e-mail, checking my eBay auctions, wrapping packages to be mailed, looking at the discussion boards for my classes on Blackboard, reading *Lost* discussion boards, showering with my fancy scented bath and body potions, and, the two biggies, my favorites: blogging and going to the gym.

This list of morning activities streamed through my head in my 2:00 p.m. waking panic.

Mind you, I have no appointments today, no pressure to be any place at any certain time. My only hard-and-fast plans, besides my daily disci- plines, is to get to the post office, work on my syllabi for my classes, and dingle around with the online classroom system.

So, why the panic? Maybe I panicked because the old me, the pre-op me, the pre–daily commitment me, might have ridden the sleep wave into depressive stagnation (where I would allow my day to be shot), mentally beat myself into a pulp, and end in a binge and the subsequent self-hatred. Sleeping in felt like old behavior.

Maybe I panicked today because I felt *out of control* for sleeping so long. Usually, I am up by 9:00 a.m. on a day like this, a day with no appoint- ments. Why the long sleep?

I called sport psychologist Dr. Rob Glibert's Success Hotline and lis- tened. It's the fifteenth anniversary of the hotline. He's been making these daily messages for public consumption for fifteen years. He mentions that people wonder how he comes up with something to say on a daily basis. He confesses that he wings it. Yep, he wings it. Gilbert justifies the winging by admonishing us to *let go of the need to be perfect*. He tells us that we don't have to get it "just right" before doing something. The *doing it*, the doing it consistently is what matters, not the supposed perfection of the thing.

He is *so* right. When I first began this blog, I only posted when I thought I had something extra meaningful to say, something emotionally hard-hitting, difficult, "worth reading." Hence, I blogged only once in a while. In my heart, I wanted to write more. I wanted to blog more often. Something inside me knew I had something to say daily. But the fear of *not being perfect* kept me from writing.

When I climbed on board for Dr. Gilbert's Thirty-Eight–Day Challenge back in November, where we were to keep a daily promise until New Year's Day, I committed to writing in this blog every day, no matter what. I'm so happy I did.

It turns out I *do* have something to say every day. Maybe it's not Pulitzer Prize–winning stuff, but it's something. It means something to me. If it's not the content of what I'm saying, then it's the daily doing of it that means something to me. I can be disciplined. I can do what I say I am going to do. I am the genuine article.

As I kept my daily commitments this early afternoon, my panic subsided. No matter what time I awaken, it doesn't matter. I'll keep my word. I'll keep my commitments. No need to panic. No need to be perfect.

If I awaken late, I can still get to the gym. It's open till 10:00 p.m. on weekdays. No big deal. No one will be there wagging their finger at me for not getting there during broad daylight. If there's too much snow on the ground and I can't get to the gym, I'll slog through a workout video and work up a sweat from my seat. I have little hand weights I can lift.

The upside of sleeping late (and there's always an upside) is that it allows me to be grateful. My body needed sleep and by the grace of God I have the schedule that permits me to get that much-needed sleep. No harm, no foul. I take care of myself. I get the sleep I need.

My left knee is feeling tender. Walking and standing on it is painful. When my garbage can is full and my buddy Matt isn't around to take it out for me, I take it out myself. This fills me with pride. Taking out my own garbage makes me feel good! Does taking out my garbage have to be painful? No. I take it to my car, which is parked close to my apartment. I put it on the hood of my car and drive it around back to the dumpster. I call it "garbage surfing."

Do what you can do. Do it every day. Let go of perfectionism. Pat yourself on the back for taking out the garbage even if you surf it there.

Want to see how far I've come and receive some free tools for your own success?

Visit LisaSargese.com

Find me on Instagram, Facebook, Twitter, and Tumblr for daily insights and inspiration so you can feel healthy and free!

January 27, 2007
THE BULLY

I'VE BEEN CALLED A "FAT pig" in my lifetime. One might think that only children on the playground could be so cruel, and they were. I was smart, loud, and awkward as a child. The tough girls in grammar school picked on me, called me "Lisa Pizza" or "Fat, Fat Water Rat." I wasn't even that heavy. I was chunky.

There was a girl who was obese, much heavier than I was. They didn't dare call her names. She would have clobbered them. She was a tomboy. I guess her brothers taught her how to fight.

I had no idea how to stick up for myself. I remember being in the gym locker room in seventh grade. I was so easy to make fun of. No one would even get near me except to abuse me. The other nerdy girls knew that they would be abused by association if they were seen with me. They kept their distance. I was a target, a target for spit balls, a target for name calling, and a target for intimidation, though they usually kept it to verbal abuse.

Well-meaning adults had told me to let the bullies' comments roll off my back like I was a duck. "Ignore them," they said. "Show them that what they're saying doesn't bother you. Be the bigger person." No one warned me that ignoring bullies can make them step up their game to get your attention.

One day, a girl named Tammy M. escalated the abuse beyond the verbal. She started with the usual name-calling, but at the advice of the grownups I ignored Tammy's verbal assault. The more I ignored her, the louder she became. She was furious with me for ignoring her.

"Hey, I'm talking to you, bitch," she bellowed as she followed me to my locker. I steeled myself against her shrill voice. Sunday school had taught me to turn the other cheek, so I did, silently ignoring her.

She reached the limit of her rage against me. She came up behind me and punched me with a closed fist in the middle of my back. I didn't stop. I didn't look at her. I just kept walking toward my locker. She punched me again.

I kept my head down and prayed that she would give up and leave me alone. She didn't.

"Look at this girl," she shrieked. "You can hit her all you want and she won't hit back!" She flailed against me as I cowered.

Someone stopped her. One of the tough girls who had known me in grammar school, Simone C., intervened for me. "Hey, leave her alone. She doesn't want to fight you. Cool it!" she said, and the onslaught stopped. I don't remember what happened next. I think I thanked Simone, but she warned me, "You need to learn to fight your own battles. I can't bail you out every time."

How could I defend myself when I had nothing inside but confusion and rage? My mother had verbally beaten any sense of self-worth out of me. At home I was silenced and controlled, shamed for the smallest of transgressions. The core issue was that I was a person at all and not merely an extension of my mother. Being an individual meant getting berated or shut out by my narcissistic mother, so I played it safe and tried not to ever be a real person.

As an adult I was still a target for bullies. I remember being in one of the loud dance clubs down at the Jersey Shore, Seaside Heights in the early 1980s. My pretty friend Mary Anne had entered and won a bikini contest. That was the year she was a contestant in the Miss New Jersey Pageant. She had a great shape. Her bikini top was made of two plastic scalloped shells like Paulina Porizkova had worn in the *Sports Illustrated Swimsuit* issue.

I was the chubby friend who held her purse and cheered from the sidelines. I was zaftig, busty, wide-assed, but well-coiffed, pretty, made- up, nice and tan from the summer sun. I didn't look like a skinny club girl, but I thought I looked nice.

She came off the stage triumphant in her bikini. As I made my way through the crowd to meet her, a muscled young guy, obviously drunk, was in my path. He turned to face me head-on, looked me up and down, and, with a disgusted sneer on his face, said, "You're a fat pig," and staggered off.

I felt humiliated. I immediately blamed myself. I told myself it was my fault for trying to fit in with the pretty people. I should have stayed back at the hotel. When I got to my friend, I kept what had just happened to myself. I didn't want to complain to her and ruin her winning moment. I smiled through my pain and snapped pictures of her.

Of course, well-meaning people, friends, and therapists told me that I shouldn't let some drunk asshole's remarks get to me. But he did get to me. I was minding my own business and he lashed out in cruelty.

When you've suffered so many insults, when people have made fun of you in childhood from day one on the playground, you learn to accept it as a given, as your lot in life, as what you deserve, and then when it happens as an adult, it just confirms that you don't measure up. No wonder I'm struggling to patch up my broken self-esteem.

So, when one of my readers posted a comment on this blog stating that sometimes she won't wear makeup because she feels like she's putting lipstick on a pig, no wonder . . . no wonder I sit hear crying till my contact lenses are foggy. No wonder I'm crying as I type this.

Does anyone have to wonder why I want to change myself? Why I want to change my appearance so I'll be more socially acceptable?

January 28, 2007

Too Tired

I'VE BEEN FEELING SLUGGISH LATELY. Kinda weak, draggy—especially after my workouts.

By the time I get home after the gym I'm usually so hungry I don't have the patience to cook or even walk to the refrigerator. I'll drop my grocery bags at my feet. I'll rip open a box of sourdough pretzels and eat till I'm queasy. An entire box contains fourteen hundred calories, and yes, I've consumed an entire box in one day. Zero grams of fat, though. That's how I justify it. No fat, no folly.

I've been working out six days a week. I've lost over eighty pounds, but now the scale isn't budging. Everyone is telling me that old cliché. I'm developing muscle, muscles weigh more than fat—*yadda, yadda*—but with this surgery, I should be dipping below three hundred pounds by now. I have no patience with plateaus. I want results.

Maybe I should form a water-drinking habit, forcing myself to drink a big glass of lemon water before enjoying my coffee in the morning. Maybe I should do some sort of daily cleansing. Nagging at the back of my mind is the notion of giving up white flour.

I resist it. I like my pretzels, I like pasta; but, I like energy and losing weight better. That's it. I've had it. I'm swearing off the white devil. No more bleached white flour. No more pretzels, not even whole-grain. No more pasta.

Am I crazy? When it comes to commitments, yeah, I'm crazy. I went to the store and bought thinly sliced turkey, sushi, tofu, shrimp, egg beaters, fat-free ricotta, fresh vegetables, fruit, yogurt, and sugar free Jell-O. I resisted buying the pretzels.

My lady friend came over for a few games of Scrabble last night. Knowing how much I like pretzels, she brought a nice big bag for us to munch on. She pulled the big bag of sourdough pretzels from her tote. I looked at them and proclaimed, out loud, "I'm off white flour, but thanks." That was tough. I really wanted those damned pretzels.

We nibbled on almonds and popcorn instead.

January 29, 2007
MOVIE POPCORN

IT'S MY FAVORITE FOOD IN the universe: movie-theater popcorn, soaked in that oil that passes itself off as butter, doused in salt and—get ready—mustard.

Yeah, gross, I know, but back in the day when I was a sweet young thing working at the popcorn stand with teens and twentysomethings at the Loews Sixplex in Secaucus, New Jersey, a customer ordered a large buttered popcorn and then asked for the mustard. We watched in horror as he glopped the mustard onto his popcorn. We were so disgusted, in fact, that as soon as he walked away we *had* to try it for ourselves. We couldn't imagine anyone actually liking mustard on their popcorn. The guy must be crazy. We tried it. It was delicious.

It was so delicious that I continued to eat popcorn that way for the next twenty years. I especially loved the theaters that had their own popcorn accessorizing stations with salt, a fake butter machine, and the obligatory mustard. The mustard was there for the hot dogs but I had my special use for it. Glop the fake butter on top in a deluge. I would actually increase the weight of my giant bag of popcorn with the amount of fake butter I applied. Then *splurp, splurp, splurp* with the mustard, in honor of my popcorn-serving days and also to ensure that no one would want to share with me. Mine, mine, mine, all mine!

Post-surgery, I dreaded going to the movie theater. I knew it would be unwise to eat the popcorn. Not only because a large bucket doused in fake butter probably contained over two thousand calories, but because I anticipated becoming grievously nauseated by what used to be my favorite food in the universe.

I postponed my first trip to the movie theater because of the popcorn issue for months—until last night. We went to see *Smokin' Aces*, a stylish bloodbath with a killer soundtrack and buckets of bullets. We went to the theater that had the glop-your-own-fake-butter machines. The once heavenly smell overwhelmed me as we entered the massive lobby of the Clifton Commons MultiPlex. I felt sick. The smell of the cooked oil was so offensive, I couldn't imagine even going near the refreshment counter. My movie mates understood. We found our seats in the theater immediately to save me the trauma of the concession stand.

Inside my purse, I had smuggled in healthy snacks: an orange pepper (that I bit into like an apple and ate to the core), an actual apple, a few fat-free Pringles, and a container of sushi.

I distracted myself with my healthy snacks. I didn't want to crave my old love. Everyone around me crunched on the oily kernels. I crunched my apple.

We sat in the front row of the ascending seats. There was a steel railing in front of us. I put my feet up on the railing. Not the tippy top of the bi-level railing, the level of the railing that was about a foot off the floor. It felt weird. Why did that feel weird? I couldn't remember a time when I had ever put my feet up like that. Why couldn't I recall ever putting my feet up?

Then, it dawned on me. I had never put my feet up because I couldn't! For so many years, I was physically unable to put my feet up on the rail. Holy crap. I *am* making progress!

I felt so normal. I felt slender, flexible, small. It felt great!

The theater filled up quickly as the movie start time approached. We were forced to sit next to each other with no seats in between us as people asked if we could move down to make room for them. To my left was a stranger, a teenage boy in his hoodie and sweatpants. As I was gathering my things so I could sit next to him, I gently tapped him and asked him to move his popcorn that was in my way. He moved it closer to him on the floor between us. It tempted me. He had eaten a handful of a giant bag of popcorn and the rest of it sat on the floor looking abandoned.

The movie started. I forgot about the stranger's bag of popcorn. I was completely captivated by the blood fest instead. The movie rocked.

When the film was over, the teenage boy and his cohorts left before the credits were over.

The uneaten popcorn was still there on the floor between us. He had hardly touched it at all. It bothered me.

I gathered my coat and purse, assembled my apple core and trash, and, just before I stood, I reached in and snatched a small handful of his popcorn. I stuffed it in my mouth. I anticipated the heavenly release of pleasure. I was disappointed. It tasted stale.

Thing is, it had always tasted stale, even all those years I had thought it was the best-tasting food in the universe. The cooked oil tasted like it had been heated, cooled, and reheated over and over. The popcorn itself was almost tasteless, like eating greasy paper. It was over. My love affair with popcorn was over. Like an abusive lover whose cheating antics and overall stupidity outweighed the security of having a so-called boyfriend, it had betrayed me for the last time.

I went home and ate another pepper.

January 31, 2007

WHERE'S THE ENERGY?

IT WAS A COMMERCIAL FOR an energy drink of some sort. It asked why we feel so let down after drinking other energy drinks. Apparently, big jolts of sugar and caffeine give a momentary boost of energy then drop us down into lethargy when they wear off.

Could that be why I get so tired lately? I've been running on fumes for over 10 years. If it wasn't for energy drinks, coffee, and my prescription for Ritalin, I would not have been able to earn two master's degrees, teach as an adjunct professor, produce a myriad of student programming, become a certified hypno-therapist, run an eBay business, keep a cozy apartment, and so on.

There were times when I dragged myself around, half-dead. I fell asleep in class. My apartment was filthy. Bills went unpaid. Deadlines were missed. I slept and napped more than my cats, but I thought that time has passed. I've been sleeping with my CPAP machine for about a year. No more sleep deprivation due to complex sleep apnea. I wake up in the morning refreshed and alert, well oxygenated.

My diabetes in under better control. My blood sugar doesn't peak in the six hundreds. I eat much less, so I'm not weighted down with binges of crappy, blank foods that cause more harm than good.

Maybe, just maybe, I don't need to overstimulate myself the way I thought I had to in the past. Maybe I don't need half a pot of coffee every morning. Maybe I don't need Ritalin to keep me alert. Maybe those sugar-free energy drinks speed me up so fast that I crash-nap when they drop me down. Maybe my fatigue is due to being up on stimulants and then dropped. Maybe I'm not as tired as I think.

I have been napping a lot lately, but I've been blaming the workouts for my fatigue and feeling betrayed that exercise hasn't given me more energy. Maybe the exercise isn't to blame. Maybe it's the yo-yo effect of the stimulants.

February 4, 2007

Pretty Face

Since I was five years old I've been getting, "Such a pretty face, if only she would lose weight." Compliments about my looks have always been conditional.

My seventeen-year-old boyfriend back in high school put his hand to my neck and told me, "You're perfect from here up." I've been passed up, rejected, insulted, left out, cheated on, yelled at, condescended to in a blur of negative reinforcement about my appearance.

Not that I'm blaming; rather, I'm naming. These things happened to me and I'm angry about them. I believe I've been treated unfairly. If I could do things over again, I would speak up for myself more, defend myself, tell people that their well-meaning comments hurt me, avoid situations where a certain "look" is required to fit in with an elitist crowd.

People can contribute to my life in a variety of ways and I to theirs. Ultimate value is not found in a dressing room mirror. I want to believe that 100 percent. I'm working so hard to be healthy, to be better. I deserve better than to be backhand complimented. Can't I just be "good" in the now, in the body I have?

February 5, 2007
THE ELEVATOR INCIDENT

FAT WOMEN TAKE A BEATING in the media and society in general. Standup comics bash us.

Red carpet interviewers don't consider us to be human. Advertisers don't use us in their ads unless we're mopping a floor, waiting on a table, nagging a man, or being the butt of a lame joke. Magazines rarely feature us, and if they do, we're a blurry, shameful mess as a celebrity's post-preg- nancy candid nightmare photo. Fat-bashing is socially acceptable.

I work at a university, and I get to eavesdrop on students' conversations daily. They speak as if no one is listening on elevators, in restrooms, on their cell phones, in class. I hear their comments about each other.

I hear the males making fun of females and each other for being "fat." I hear females calling themselves and each other horrible, judgmental names for not looking like a tiny celebrity. It's out there. Fat prejudice is alive and kicking, kicking me right in my self-esteem. It hurts to hear offhand comments against fat people.

I was waiting for the elevator with a crowd of students. I wasn't going to squish into the next available elevator. I planned to take the next one after that. It arrived. As most of the crowd ahead of me piled into the elevator, the elevator that I had no intention of boarding, two tall, young, athletic-looking males joked to each other as they were the last ones to fit into the elevator car. They joked that the car was full to capacity and that "anyone approaching three hundred pounds shouldn't try to get on." Then one said to the other, "*Approaching?*"

Now, I don't know if they were looking at me, joking about me, or if they were poking fun at one another. It was their conversation. They weren't terribly loud nor were they aiming their remarks at anyone. Regardless, I was offended.

Here I am, trying so hard, working every day to fight my demons, pushing, pushing pushing, so the scale will dip below the three hundred mark and I have to hear that sh*t? But saying something to them would have made me feel like an eavesdropping psycho. I would have felt paranoid and downright obnoxious if I had said something in response to their comments. It's such a gray area, the "Should I say something or not?" dilemma.

I wonder, if their comment was racist, would there be a dilemma?

February 23, 2007

FAST APPLE AND DAD

AFTER THE GYM, I WENT to my parents' house, a one-minute drive from my own apartment. I stopped in to visit with my father who was just waking up from a nap. He met me in the kitchen. I was eating an after-workout snack that I thought was beyond reproach, an apple—a good one, too. It was nice and crisp and sweet, cold from my parents' refrigerator.

It wasn't a reward. I was hungry. I had just worked out. I had pushed myself to do my five minutes on the elliptical even though I didn't feel like it. For most of my thirty minutes on the stationary bike, I dreaded the five minutes on the elliptical stepper. I tried to rationalize my way out of doing it. I thought I might do five minutes on the treadmill instead. But doing the right thing, keeping my word, proved to be the more satisfying choice. My sense of accomplishment and self-esteem beamed and glowed in the aftermath.

My dad sat with me in the kitchen and found me enjoying that nice, cold apple. I told him proudly that I was "up to eighty-four pounds." What did I mean by that, he asked. Weight loss, I informed him. I've lost a total of eighty-four pounds. His reaction was lukewarm. He looked like he didn't believe me. I told myself that he was just waking up and must be a little foggy. I couldn't expect him to jump up and down and cheer for me or lavish me with praise, right? Poor man was tired.

We talked as I ate. My father is the one who buys the fruit for the household. I commented on what a good apple it was, figuring that showing him appreciation and praise for having selected it at the fruit stand might make him feel good. Rather than keep silent about the good things in life, I try to put positivity out in the world. When something's good, I say it's good. He batted off the compliment by saying he didn't even know what kind of apple it was. Then he made the comment. A comment from one's father has a certain impact. I took it personally. I took it hard.

He said with disdain, "I had no idea you could eat an apple that fast."

Guilty. I was guilty. How dare I eat an apple at a hungry pace! I had the gastric bypass surgery. I should be eating applesauce, because that's what people expect of me. Should I be OK with eating an apple and three—count 'em—three raw peppers for dinner? Shame on me!

The other day I told my shrink that I eat fresh fruits and vegetables most of the time. She said, "You cook them, of course, right?" Um . . . no. I eat them raw. They make me less nauseated that way. C'mon people! Isn't that how you're supposed to eat fruits and vegetables to get the most nutrition out of them? What's with all the comments?

I tried to enjoy my apple. My father looked disgusted. My apple eating was defying his sense of expectation. The look on his face made me feel like an apple glutton. I made an excuse, a true excuse, but a justification nonetheless. I said, "Yes, I can eat an apple. I can eat raw fruits and vegetables. But if I eat just one potato chip, I'll be deathly sick." I felt I owed him that reassurance. He wasn't satisfied. He scowled at me. His doubt of my ability to respect my surgery was glaring at me. I was crestfallen. I'm doing everything right and yet I felt so wrong.

My stomach is normal-size. Normal for me means I eat appropriate serving sizes. I don't vomit. I don't choke on fried rice because I don't eat fried rice. I don't hawk up McDonald's hamburgers and fries because my stomach pouch is too small or because I wolfed it down too fast. I don't eat fast food at all!

I feel like I'm eating a healthier diet than most of the American population. I don't even eat pasta any longer. The only white food I eat is the rice that comes with my sushi. I've turned my life around. There's no junk food in my life, and I don't crave it or miss it.

I eat when I'm hungry and stop when I'm full. I eat *tons* of raw fruits and vegetables. My snacks are yogurt, almonds, and sugar-free Jell-O. My desserts are sugar-free ice pops and sugar-free Jell-O pudding. I take in sixty grams or more of lean protein per day.

I'm born again hard! And yet, people are fucking with me. Maybe it's time to get angry. Maybe my passive acceptance of their comments is karmically wrong. Perhaps it's time to be polite, compassionate, but firm with people. Not just because they need to be put in their place, but because their words are hurting me. Why should I absorb that kind of energy rather than deflecting it?

Why should I tolerate unsavory, disheartening comments because people mean well? My tiny little stomach is meant to internalize food not careless comments or my own anger.

I left without saying anything to my father.

March 1, 2007

FATHER AND THE APPLE CHEWING

I'M CATCHING MY BREATH AFTER a good sob. Why? My father doesn't like the way I chew.

After the apple-eating incident, after I'd left my parents' house, my father asked my mother, "When is she going to stop chewing that way?" And then he mockingly imitated me. He imitated my chewing.

How do I know this? Because my mother, in her infinite capacity for evil, told me! She even imitated the way he was imitating me. The tears flooded out of me. She started to cry as she watched me standing in the cold outside her car, sobbing. Maybe she's not totally without empathy. She cried because she felt bad for me, but then again she was happy bcause she succeeded in making me angry at my father.

I'm laughing now, thinking of the caveman in the GEICO commercial. He's sitting with his therapist and he gets a call on his cell phone. He says, "My mother's calling. I'll put it on speaker."

I feel cleansed after my heaving sob fest. Crying is a wonderful way to clear out stale, rotten emotional residue. Crying over my father's insensitivity and my mother's cruelty helped me to get over myself and realize that I have a choice. I can dwell on what he said and play it over and over in my mind while feeling miserable, or I can go to the gym and earn some self-respect.

I'll choose the latter.

March 2, 2007

"I Will Not Let Thee Go, Except Thou Bless Me"

There's a girl at the gym who works out rather hard. She wears her blonde hair in a ponytail. It swishes back and forth like a windshield wiper against her back when she runs on the treadmill.

I've seen her at the gym a few times. I'd never seen a female do chin-ups before. She does many chin-ups. She's strong. I've watched her move with determination from machine to free weights to treadmill. She's one of the few who actually runs on the treadmill. In addition to running, she side-hops on the treadmill. I didn't even know that was possible. She has a Hollywood figure, taut and toned. Her freckles are sprinkled generously across her body. She's pretty and perky. She's the anti-Lisa. It seemed that whenever she passed near me, she would contort her body a bit to avoid touching me. I wanted to tell her, "Hey, the fat isn't catching!" She must think I'm gross.

I wasn't looking good at the gym yesterday. The tears from my father's thoughtless criticism were fresh on my face. I'd grabbed any old stretchy clothes from the quagmire of my bedroom floor. They were swimming on me, draping me in unflattering waves of mismatched fabrics in brown, black, and blue. I looked like a bruise. When I walked from the parking lot to the gym, I passed a gorgeous sky-blue, vintage

T-Bird. Ponytail blonde crossed my mind. It seemed like the kind of car she would drive. Pretty, shiny, and perfect, like a Barbie car.

She wasn't inside the gym when I arrived, but came in a few minutes later. I tried not to stare. Her look is so remarkable. Her arm and lower back sport tattoos, punctuating her tight, athletic frame. I envied her. She ran on the treadmill as I pedaled on my stationary bike. I pedaled furiously, and I don't mean that as a metaphor. I was angry at my father. My anger fueled my workout and turbocharged my ferocity. I glanced at my reflection in the mirror. I felt like warm clay that needed to be molded. I glanced at her and the swinging blonde ponytail and fell into the trap of comparing myself to her. She was the summit. I pedaled, hacking my way up the mountain toward her impossible ideal.

I didn't want her to see me looking at her. It's bad gym etiquette to stare. I sat there, pedaling, stewing in my acidic anger. I felt like the queen alien from *Aliens*, hissing as my giant abdomen plopped out another slimy, venomous egg. She was Ripley with a flamethrower, ready to extinguish me as the lesser drone aliens backed out of the egg room with their heads lowered in fear.

I hauled my alien shape through my workout routine. I worked and perspired. Ponytail girl worked hard, her lifting and chin-upping accompanied by girlish grunts. I judged her. I thought she was a snob. I thought her life must be so much easier than mine. I thought she was privileged. My thoughts were unkind.

As I was thinking of her unkindly, I thought of my students. I imagined telling them that I was intimidated and fascinated by her, that I believed I was too gross to be near her, that she would never talk to me. I thought about promising them that I would introduce myself to her someday, that I would get up the nerve and soften her heart with my sincerity and praise, telling her how much she had inspired me. How could I teach about Buddhism, nonjudgment, and compassion and then think so critically of a stranger? I silently vowed that someday I'd get to know her. I'd stop judging her. *Someday*, I thought. *Someday*.

My routine was almost over. She was getting ready to work on a machine just two feet away from me. She was so close. This untouchable beauty, a red-carpet starlet to be admired safely from afar, was arm's length from me. I couldn't help myself. I looked at her. Our eyes met. She surprised me. She spoke to me, saying, "You're doing a great job, really. Keep up the good work. You're an inspiration."

The world began to melt. Her voice was small but solid. Her sincerity beamed from her blue eyes. I stammered a thank you and something about having lost ninety-two pounds. Her eyes were intent. She continued, "I just had to let you know what an inspiration you are. What's your name?"

She stuck out her hand to shake mine. I was timid and said my hand was sweaty. "Don't worry, so is mine," she reassured.

She said her name is Sean. (When I got home, I looked it up. It's an Irish name meaning "God's gracious gift.") I told her she made my day. "Keep it up!" she told me.

My insides felt as if they were turning to liquid. I didn't sob, but the tears poured steadily from my eyes in hot streams. They blended with my sweat, or so I hoped. I didn't want to embarrass her with my tears. It wasn't a gaspy cry. I didn't sniffle. The hot tears simply flowed.

I couldn't look her in the eye again. I hurriedly finished my workout and lunged for the exit door. Then I let it out. A sob fest on the way to my car. I huffed. I sniffed. The second big cry of the morning. God's gracious gift had blessed me. I rejoiced.

Sean, God's gracious gift, had blessed me. I was humbled. She was the one to approach me! I didn't have to set a goal to meet her—she broke into my world, like divine grace. She was the one who was inspired by me! It was unsettling. My father's cruel comment still hung heavy on my heart, though, tainting my gracious experience with Sean.

I went to see my father. I cried and choked out my displeasure with his comment about me. He raged at my mother for repeating what he had said about the way I chewed. He alternately pounded things as he yelled at her and begged my forgiveness. I cried some more then left.

It was over. The pain of anticipation was over, the pain of dreading a conversation with Sean and the pain of knowing I had to confront my father. Not only was the pain over, but I had been blessed.

Blessed by Sean, God's gracious gift, and blessed by my father's regret over hurting me.

Funny thing about Sean, when I finally got to talking to her I found out she's a divorced mother of three who has her own personal fitness business. She struggles to make ends meet. She told me she has to work out extra hard to stay in shape, because she has to compete with younger, fitter trainers.

March 31, 2007
THE NAZI AND THE BRAID

My FRIEND, ROMA, TOLD ME a story about how her mother escaped Poland during the Nazi invasion. The Nazi soldiers rounded up Jews and other non-Aryans in her village near the Polish border. Roma's mother (Roma had not been born yet) was among them. She and others were corralled in a local church to await transport to one of the "work" camps. Roma described her mother as being beautiful with a long, thick braid of dark hair trailing from under her kerchief down the middle of her back. She tended to the elderly, the sick, and the children who were confined in the church under Nazi guard. She fetched water. She soothed and comforted. She distributed what little food there was.

A young Nazi soldier watched her as she made her way from person to person, from family to family. Roma said, "He watched her, following that long braid of hers with his eyes as she tended to the needy." Her compassion touched his heart. He fell in love with her instantly. He couldn't keep his eyes off her braid, a symbol of all that was good and kind in the world.

At night, he pulled her away from the sleeping prisoners and took her outside. He pointed toward an unguarded area that would lead her to the border. "Run," he told her. "Run, and don't look back."

She protested. There were people in need. He told her that if she stayed, she would be dead by the next evening as they were all destined for the gas chamber. He told her he couldn't bear to see her die. He shoved her onto the dark path with the butt of his gun. With tears in his eyes, he told her to go or he would shoot her there where she stood.

She ran for her life as he watched that braid disappear into the night forever.

Roma told me that story over twelve years ago. I haven't seen her since, but I never forgot that story.

I've always longed for someone to notice me that way—my compassion, my hard work. I want to be that good. I want to be so kind someone falls in love with my kindness. Usually, I'm tough, independent, my own best company, but that is not always the case. Sometimes I wish to be noticed, to be loved like that. I've wondered if someone would ever be captivated by me, fall in love with me, looking longingly at my "braid."

March 29, 2007

When the sleep center diagnosed my complex sleep apnea—the way my throat closes and my breathing stops during sleep—it was so severe, the technician almost called the emergency room to revive me during the sleep test. I was only breathing 60 percent of the time. My brain was oxygen-starved. My heart raced and paused, then kick-started itself. I hadn't had a good night's sleep in years. My very life was at risk. No wonder I was hooked on caffeine and Ritalin.

This diagnosis was given a year ago. I've been sleeping with a CPAP machine ever since. I remember telling my mother about the experience in the sleep lab, how severe my condition was, and how I'd been suffering for years. I wanted sympathy. I wanted her to tell me how incredibly strong I was to have accomplished so much while living with this debilitating condition. I wanted her to be thankful I was alive.

Maybe she misunderstood the seriousness of living with untreated sleep apnea. The risk of heart attack and stroke should have startled her. The fact that her daughter was oxygen-starved should have concerned her. The fact that lack of sleep contributes to the body's inability to shed fat should have alarmed her. Her response: "What, you think you're supposed to get eight hours of sleep per night? I never sleep for a full eight hours and look how hard I work! Nobody sleeps eight hours a night. That's not a disorder! Nobody sleeps through the night!"

Looking back, I tell myself that she simply didn't understand. My mother has low tolerance for other people's ailments. She doesn't believe there is such a thing as postpartum depression, for instance. She doesn't have patience with my seventy-six-year-old father when he's too tired to shovel snow all day. She doesn't believe in resting when you're sick. Sickness is for the lazy and weak-willed. That's the way she is. If you need and receive sympathy, she thinks you're being coddled. Since she never received the sympathy and support she needed as a child, her wounds are so deep she's incapable of giving sympathy and support to others. It's a symptom of her narcissistic personality disorder.

Even though I understand that she's unable to sympathize, I felt hurt. I felt misunderstood. She totally invalidated me. I had gone to the hospital for help. That was hard enough. Finding out that I had a dangerous condition that was slowly killing me (along with the diabetes and crippling fat) was frightening. Discovering that my $4000-plus hospital bill for the apnea diagnosis was 100 percent *not* covered by insurance was panicking me. Didn't the insurance company want me to live?

Good thing I have friends who support me. Thank God they showed me appropriate concern. But, I still blamed myself for my own ailment. When you're raised a certain way, it's difficult to unlearn what you have learned. When I'm sick, I have to force myself to be kind and to take a healing stance with myself rather than let the old habits of self-blame kick in. It's difficult when you have a mother who makes you feel indulgent for getting necessary medical care.

April 10, 2007

SELF-MUTILATION

I'M DISTURBED. I'M DISTURBED BY the number of women who have contacted me saying they identify with my blog post where I discuss picking at my skin.

They've said things like, "I find places on my body to attack." Or, "I won't let scabs heal, I'll just keep picking at them." Or, "I dig into my scalp with my fingernails till it bleeds."

What are we doing to ourselves? Disturbing as the habit itself is the way it's hidden from society. Eating disorders make tabloid headlines. Body-image issues fill the pages of women's magazines, but this skin- picking, self-mutilation thing? I think it's an epidemic, a closet epidemic.

I tried to get professional help. A few years ago, I was in session with my therapist. I told her that I thought I might be a self-mutilator. Her response? "Oh, you are not," and she dropped the subject. I guess she had seen such severe cases that the blood under my fingernails and polka-dot scars all over my thighs and torso were not enough to be worth her attention. I didn't pursue the conversation.

My mother had done a similar thing to me. Back when I was sixteen, I was bulimic. I was a binge-purge bulimic who didn't lose any weight. Since my goal was to become thin and that didn't happen, I blamed myself for not being able to vomit up enough of my food. My pattern was binge, purge, binge, purge, binge, then collapse with a semi-full stomach, exhausted from the vomiting. My mother heard me throwing up one night after dinner. It's hard to cover up the sound of gagging and food splashing into the toilet. When I emerged from the bathroom, she yelled, "You're not gonna start that sh*t are you? Ohhh, no. Don't you dare!" She was annoyed with me. There was no sympathy in her voice, no caring. She wasn't concerned, just angry. Her yelling didn't make me stop. It just made me transfer my vomiting episodes to my bedroom, where I'd use jars, bags, dishes, or whatever, then dispose of the purge waste later, unbeknownst to my mother.

So, when my therapist dismissed my little cry for help, it fit right in with my self-image of someone with an imaginary disorder that was too much trouble for anyone to care about. My sickness was an annoyance. I kept it to myself.

As a teenager, a beautiful teenager, I constantly picked at my face. I had mild acne—probably not even diagnosable as acne, just some pimples. They disgusted me. I'd pick and squeeze at them until my face was blotched with bloody, scabby pulp. My boyfriend at the time would sarcastically tell me to keep on picking and gouging. He was the same boyfriend who, when I started to gain weight, told me that he was going to fill me with helium and float me in the Thanksgiving Day parade. I guess he thought shaming me would change me. It didn't.

I should be crying as I write this, but I'm not. Surviving these horrible disorders has made me strong. Not so strong that I don't need help; rather, strong enough to go out in the world and find the help I need, strong enough to know my own mind and what it needs to heal itself, strong enough to admit that I need care from people who can actually give it to me.

Sometimes that's our problem. We isolate ourselves. We're ashamed of our eating, bingeing, purging, digging, gouging, and we hide away, certain that we're the only ones who do it and certain that we're too disgusting to be in anyone's company or to seek encouragement and understanding from our fellow human beings. Shame and isolation keep us sick. I know this blog is good for people, because you've written to me telling me you feel less alone and ashamed because of what I shared.

A few years ago, I started to notice the thoughts I was having while picking at myself.

This took discipline since the actual habit was automatic. I would zone out, oblivious to anyone who was in the room with me or, worse yet, maintain conversation with them while my hand roamed all over my body looking for zits to pick, imperfections to excise. Sometimes people would notice and give an uncomfortable glance at my hand but never say anything.

What I observed is that any time I was picking, I happened to be thinking of ways that I fell short of my perfectionist self-expectations or when I was experiencing self-doubt. I might be replaying a conversation in my head, one where I wished I had said something differently. I might be rehearsing a conversation in my head that was yet to take place and anticipating a negative response from my imaginary interlocutor. I might be thinking about how I wish I had handled a situation differently. I might be thinking of good things, positive things, and when the self-doubt crept in, when the negative voice piped in, the picking would start. I've also associated the picking with a feeling of cleaning out, digging at my pores to try to exorcise the demons of my imperfections.

Dear God, can this be helped? What I observed must be so for others. I'm sure this disorder has symptoms and features just like any other disorder. It must be diagnosable and treatable.

April 30, 2007

LOVE YOUR ENEMIES

I STARTED SUNDAY SCHOOL AT five years old and attended dutifully every week. We learned that Jesus taught us to love our enemies. He said we should turn the other cheek. I believed that was the way I was supposed to live my life.

As a kid on the playground I was name-called and bullied, beginning in first grade. On the first-grade playground, there was kid named Vincent. He picked on me in the mornings before school. He was the terror of the playground. I don't quite remember what he called me, but he called me names. He made fun of me. He yelled. He pushed me when the playground monitor wasn't looking. I was told by other kids that nobody likes a tattletale, so I didn't report him. No, he wasn't "dipping my pigtails in the inkwell" or flirting with me in a boyish way. He was a bully. He was being mean to me because he could be. He was one of those bullies who got a kick out of the way I wouldn't fight back. I just took the abuse.

I dreaded my playground time in the mornings before class. Whatever names he called me, I remember feeling hurt. I remember how disgusted he sounded when he yelled at me—such vitriol. I believed the things he said. I felt disgusting. I hadn't done anything to antagonize him. He just sensed that I was weak and that I wouldn't defend myself. That's what bullies do.

I was a good girl—obedient, polite. If Sunday school taught me to "turn the other cheek" and forgive, then that's what I would do. I was supposed to love my enemies, so I would try to love Vincent. That's what Jesus taught. That's what God wanted. Surely, the power of love would change his heart. So when Christmas time came around, I made Vincent a Christmas card. I wanted him to know that I forgave him for making me dread the morning playground time. I wanted him to feel loved and understood. I wanted to show him that despite his cruelty, I found something deserving about him. It was Christmas and he should know that he was forgiven and loved. I told no one I was doing this. I made the card myself at home.

We were outside on the black tar playground in the December cold. He still had the energy to yell and scream ugly taunts at me despite the frigid weather. I interrupted his racing around. He stopped, surprised as I handed him the card. He took it. He looked at it. "What is this?" he demanded.

"It's a Christmas card for you, Vincent." I answered proudly, hoping his heart would melt at my forgiveness and generosity. "Is it from you?" he asked impatiently.

"Yes. From me to you." I smiled.

He frowned. "I don't want this piece of garbage," he said and ripped the card to pieces. He threw the shreds in my face and ran away.

I didn't blame him. I figured I hadn't loved my enemy in the way Jesus wanted me to. I vowed to myself to pay better attention in Sunday school.

May 1, 2007
Friggin' Scale

Why did the scale say 279? In a recent blog post, I said I didn't believe in plateaus and now the universe is testing me. My most recent "low" on the scale was 274, making my total weight loss since August 103 pounds. I'm still 150 pounds overweight according to my surgeon; therefore, my plateau means I'm a failure.

If I were talking to a client, I would counsel them about the scale being unreliable. I would insist that the body changes and adjusts with peaks and dips in weight. That if you plot the numbers on a graph, as long as the overall trend is a decrease in weight, then everything is fine.

I would talk about muscle weighing more than fat. I'd be reassuring. But for me? For me, I'm going to beat myself up and scrutinize my every morsel. Looking at my exercise routine, I've been missing the strength- training portion of my workouts. I've done my forty-five minutes of cardio six days a week, but I get to the weight training maybe just two or three days a week. I've been using the cardio setting on the treadmill and bikes rather than the fat-burn setting because I wanted to push myself harder, so I've been too tired to do the weights after the bike.

Money's been tight. My cupboard is not as well stocked as it should be. There have been days when I've eaten foods made of white flour—a bagel, a roll. Cheap food. This little laundry list of failures is my rationalization for the uncooperative scale. Damn me and damn that scale.

May 7, 2007

Normal on a Sunday

IT WAS SO NORMAL, a small miracle of normalcy. My Sunday companion and I walked down the hill from my apartment to the flea market in the park at the end of my block. We meandered. We bargained. We admired.

We desired. We contemplated antiques, talked ourselves into and out of buying things we didn't need.

When we were more than halfway through the park I had my revelation. My Sunday companion had run across the street to the cash machine to fetch a wad of bills for a sterling silver item that couldn't possibly be left behind. I plopped myself down in the warm grass, turned my face up to the sun. And then it dawned on me. I had just *walked* the entire length of the park. Walking outdoors in the Sunday sunshine had been my idea in the first place.

A year ago, this would not have happened. I would never have suggested an outdoor activity. I would *never* have suggested *any* activity that required walking farther than the distance between the car and the front door. I would have been in terrible pain from even standing at those flea market tables let alone walking around them.

Even choosing to sit on the ground was a big deal, a milestone of normalcy. I sat because I was just a little bit fatigued. I was fatigued in the same way that the other shoppers were. The same way normal people feel after walking through half the park. Sitting in the grass was simply miraculous, miraculously normal. Last year I wouldn't have been able to lower myself to the ground, and I'd have never been able to get myself up to a standing position without a hoist and a winch.

Our walk in the park was a small but significant triumph. Who would have thought I'd ever celebrate becoming normal?

May 15, 2007

Revisiting Lady Liberty

I NEVER THOUGHT I'D SEE her again. She looks more beautiful now than ever, pale green and majestic against a perfectly sunny sky. The Statue of Liberty looked me directly in the eyes and reassured me. Her proud, calm expression seemed to ask, "If I'm still here, why wouldn't you be?"

As stalwart as I am, I always harbored a little doubt. A small place inside me knew that in spite of my strong life force, my death drive could win at any moment. I had allowed myself to become dangerously sick and nearly lethally diabetic. Walking was agony. I remembered what hope felt like but couldn't muster much of it. That's how I felt the last time I saw the Statue of Liberty a few years ago. It felt like it might be my last. Part of me was saying goodbye to her, to New York Harbor, to life. I really was ready to die.

That's why I insisted that I take my mother on the *Spirit of New Jersey* this past Sunday for their Mother's Day cruise. It was my idea. Don't get me wrong—Mom loves the ship. She loves cruising, but more so to show off to her guests who've never sailed before rather than to actually enjoy for herself. She loves taking out-of-towners on the cruises and giving her special narration of all the sights in the harbor. She talks about how she was "the floor show" a few years ago—ten years ago maybe?—when she was still able to dance and draw attention to herself on the dance floor, before the arthritis set in. Cruising for her own enjoyment with only me as an audience is not very satisfying to her, but I insisted.

It had been years since I could actually enjoy being on the ship. I wanted to use my newfound energy and take my lighter body for a test drive. I wanted to climb the steps to the observation deck. I wanted to hop up on my feet from our brunch table inside the ship and walk outside to the stern to get a closer look at the Statue of Liberty, and that's exactly what I did this Sunday. "C'mon, Ma. C'mon, Ma. C'mon, Ma, we're getting closer. We have to make our way outside to see her," I urged as the ship approached Liberty Island. She walks with a cane, so it takes her a little bit of time to get from the table to the outside deck.

Once we were outside, my mother tried to steal the moment as she often tries to do. She grimaced through her drama tears and squealed about how every time she sees the Statue of Liberty she remembers her sister, Mae, her favorite sister who has since passed away and who once enjoyed this very cruise with my mother. Do I mean to say my mother doesn't mourn for Mae? Of course she does. You'd have to see her in action in order to understand her exaggerated way of drawing attention to herself. She's a moment stealer. She wanted our seeing Lady Liberty to be about her. Her memories. Her Statue of Liberty. It was Mother's Day—I let her have her moment. I put my hand reassuringly on her back, rubbed her a bit, and said, "I know, Ma, I know."

But I wouldn't defer to her entirely. There we were standing on the stern of our harbor cruise ship, the engines cut down to a low purr as we slid past Lady Liberty, an insistent wind chilling us on an otherwise perfect spring day, and I started to cry. Quietly, sincerely, hot tears clouded my eyes. I prayed silently to the mighty Statue of Liberty, the lady-lighthouse with her tireless arm, taut and muscular, raised triumphantly in the air as if to say, "Lisa, I knew I'd see you again. I knew you could do it. Just as sure as I'm standing, I knew."

I wasn't sure I'd see her again. That's why I was crying. As determined as I was, I knew it could have gone a different way. I knew I could easily have died of a heart attack, stroke, or pneumonia. Sleep apnea could have killed me in my sleep, too, and I didn't even know I suffered from it back then.

But I lived. I lived hard. I stood there crying up to Lady Liberty and thought of every time I didn't feel like going to the gym or doing that extra five minutes on the treadmill. I thought of pushing myself to do my weight training when I wasn't in the mood. This is the payoff, I thought. Looking into the eyes of a silent guardian with her arm in the air, in solidarity and knowing how persistence saved my life. It brought me back to the Hudson River, to our lady of hope standing persistently in the harbor. I lived, Lady. I lived.

May 27, 2007
BINGE EATING

I STILL EAT TOO MUCH sometimes, but now instead of "too much" being one whole pizza or three types of Entenmann's cakes, "too much" is two yogurts or two apples instead of one. I do much less damage to myself now, but the need to fill the emptiness is still there.

I remember the days of going to the Quick Check to buy three Entenmann's cakes, plus some half-and-half and maybe some Sweet'N Low to make it look like I was buying supplies for company that's dropping by unexpectedly. I remember the Saturday nights I would park in front of my apartment and eat all three cakes in the car alone. I remember the drive-thru days. I would spend close to twenty dollars at the Burger King drive-thru. Eat it all in the car, then go to the McDonald's drive-thru and eat there, too.

Back in the day (less than a year ago) I would order sixty-five dollars' worth of Italian delivery food—pizzas, eggplant parmesan, pasta, garlic bread, and salad (for some god unknown reason I wanted some fiber in my diet) and wash it all down with two liters of diet soda loaded with tons of ice to cool down my pitifully agonized stomach. When I gave a talk the other night, someone asked me if I could really eat two whole pizzas and a gallon and a half of ice cream in one sitting. Of course I could and two sleeves of Lorna Doones, a couple of bags of chips, and half a jar of chunky peanut butter. Peanut butter and jelly sandwiches were a favorite binge food. I could eat an entire loaf of bread, a jar of peanut butter, and a jar of jelly and wash it all down with a half-gallon of chocolate milk.

This surprises people, but I lived like this for years. Part of me was trying to die. Part of me was trying to live, to self-medicate with food. Part of me was trying to fill the emptiness. It was like throwing a handful of pennies into the Grand Canyon and hoping it would fill up like a piggy bank. Bottomless. Never ending. Echoing emptiness. All the peanut butter and jelly in the world couldn't fill me. The only reason my binges would come to an end was that I became exhausted and unable to eat any more physically, though emotionally I wanted more.

I would eat to the point of paralysis. I would collapse on the sofa with my heart racing, my stomach stretched out and in terrible pain, nauseated, and with near-lethal levels of blood sugar.

It was never enough. Never.

I still eat too much, but now "too much" is a few too many handfuls of almonds or an extra container of yogurt. The feeling is still the same, though. I feel full, bloated, paralyzed, nauseated—only now I'm not killing myself. This way I am only so full, but I still have the ability to feel something, like sadness, loneliness, anger, fear . . . fear of sadness, loneliness, anger, fear itself.

For all this suffering and surgery, I'm still eating to the point of pain.

May 28, 2007

BEACH MEMORIES AND DREAD

I WASN'T LOOKING FORWARD TO decorating my door. As a matter of fact, I was dreading it. My apartment door is always decorated for the season. For spring, I hang a little felt banner of a lady bug climbing a flower. For Valentine's Day, I hang a giant heart. Christmas gets a wreath. Pumpkins and witches for Halloween, a big turkey in November. Mine is a festive door. This weekend, it's time to hang a flag and some red, white, and blue ribbons and bows.

Memorial Day officially begins my favorite season, summer. I think after years of conditioning, I learned to love summer best because it meant that I didn't have to go to school. I loved school—the classroom part, the learning part. I was good at learning. School was where I got to excel and garner attention and praise from my teachers far from the denigrating influence of my mother, but being bullied was so very painful.

I hated the playground. I hated gym. I hated being picked on by the other kids. I hated being made fun of and not knowing how to defend myself. I had no peace as a kid. The other kids tormented me at school, then my mother tormented me at home. I had nowhere to run and hide except to be silent in my room so as not to draw my mother's annoyance or wrath. As a kid, summer meant that I would only have to deal with one demon, the more familiar demon, the mother demon, and leave the playground demons behind till the fall.

I have lots of great memories from the summer, like my parents taking me down to the Jersey Shore for the day. They fought, but not too badly. They tried hard to get along for just one day for "the kid's" sake. My mother orchestrated the day according to her understanding of the reality. We would leave at 6:00 a.m. to avoid the traffic. Arriving at Point Pleasant before the beaches were even open, we'd stop at a certain pancake house that was always open early, a little mom-and-pop joint one block off the beach. My father would get his coffee, my mother her Sanka. Shore day was a special occasion, so I was allowed to eat a giant stack of pancakes with gobs of syrup and butter, bacon, and chocolate milk instead of regular milk. My little stomach ached from the overeating, but my parents were getting along, so I was happy. As long as they were eating, they weren't fighting, and I was allowed to indulge myself. It was bliss.

We'd always go to Risden's Beach and get lockers for the day. The old man who worked there recognized my parents and our '67 convertible Chevy year after year. He and my father bonded over how "great the car looks every time I see it" and how big the "little girl" was getting. Dad was in a good mood when he received compliments on his car. Mother was proud. Little Lisa was stuffed full of pancakes and happy.

On the beach itself, we never ate boardwalk food. Back in the day, folks were allowed to bring a picnic onto the beach. My mother always packed the same lunch for me: a bologna sandwich on Arnold's white bread with Hellmann's mayonnaise and a side of green grapes. For years as an adult, a loaf of Arnold's, a jar of Hellmann's, and a pound of bologna would be a favorite binge—to hell with the grapes.

My mother took good care of me on shore days. She was proud of herself for anticipating all our needs as she pulled foods and drinks out of the cooler like Mary Poppins pulling magic out of her carpet bag. At around 4:00 p.m., we would retire to the lockers, take an uncomfortably cold shower to get all the sand off, and dress for dinner. I remember the comforting smell of Shower To Shower bath powder and the feeling of being sandless and dry after an itchy day on the beach. The fresh cotton underwear sealed in the cushy comfort.

We'd eat at a seafood restaurant on the boardwalk. Sometimes negotiating where to eat would spark a fight between my parents. My father was hungry and cranky. My mother was contentious and controlling. I was anxious to get to the restaurant so Dad could have his cocktail. They'd force themselves to get along for the duration of the meal while I stuffed myself with bread and butter and some heavy, cheese-laden entree.

After dinner, we'd stroll the boardwalk and I'd go on the kiddie rides— alone. As an only child, I was used to sitting alone in the little train car or the roller coaster car or the Tilt-A-Whirl seat. I'd go around and around and wave to my parents as I passed them, hoping they weren't fighting in my absence. Because my mother wanted it, we'd get a walk-away sundae or some other sugary treat before we piled back into the Chevy for the long ride home. My mother had that orchestrated, too. She'd dress me in my pajamas and lay down a clean, cool sheet on the back seat so the houndstooth upholstery wouldn't feel rough on my sunburned legs. I'd always fall asleep before we arrived home. Dad would carry me inside.

Years later, as a fat adult, I dreaded going down the shore. I wasn't fit enough to walk on the sand properly. Going past ankle depth in the ocean tired me out. I dreaded the ability to choose my own foods. I couldn't trust myself. I always overate to the point of pain. I dreaded the imminent failure to eat moderately. Smelling the hot vanilla from the sugary boardwalk foods was too much for me. I always ate too much, trying to regain the good feelings from childhood. The good feelings never came.

Decorating my apartment door was a safe thing to do to celebrate the season, yet I dreaded it. Why was I dreading the door decorating? Pain. I dreaded the pain. In the past, standing at my front door was a Herculean effort. Standing made me out of breath. Going into my closet to get the bag of seasonal decorations was an effort. Standing hurt, reaching hurt, bending over to get the hammer hurt, standing at the front door arranging the flags and banners hurt. My legs, my knees, my back, my lungs were all on fire from the exertion. Decorating meant suffering. For years, I suffered as I decorated, but I did it because the result cheered me up.

This time, when I opened the closet to fetch the flag, I was fine. I wasn't out of breath, I wasn't in any pain, it was no big deal to bend over to get the hammer. Standing at the front door was no big deal. Nothing hurt. I breathed easily. The dread was just a habit. Dreading the effort was an old habit, conditioned by years of pain and suffering.

I'm free to enjoy the shore again now. The decisions about food are made for me. If I ate a walk-away sundae now, I'd be so sick to my stomach. Blech! The thought of eating greasy, heavy boardwalk food is a big turnoff. It's not even tempting. My body signals nausea at the thought of it. I never have to dread the temptation ever again. Never. I made the big decision to have the surgery so that all subsequent decisions would be made in my favor.

I could take a bite or two of a walk-away sundae and that's it. No more stuffing myself with junk food. Not now, not ever. Eating to the point of pain and nausea? Yes, unfortunately. But eating too much for my caloric needs? No, it's not even an option.

May 29, 2007

MY GASTRIC BANDING STORY BEFORE
THERE WAS SUCH A THING AS A LAP BAND

IN 1988, I WAS ONE of the first recipients of the adjustable gastric band as a patient of Dr. Lubomyr Kuzmak who practiced in New Jersey. The FDA was in the process of approving the adjustable gastric band for use beyond the experimental stage. Mine was installed during the experimental stage. My band had to be replaced in 1993 after leaking out all of its saline, rendering it unable to be adjusted. I received a second gastric band, FDA approved and improved. The port flipped over after surgery and rendered the band nonadjustable. I lived with it inside me for another thirteen years. This type of weight-loss surgery is now called the lap band, indicating that it is surgically installed via laparoscopy. Both of my banding surgeries were done with full incision, not laparoscopy.

My mother will sometimes try to make me admit that I did something "stupid," and I put the word in quotes because, yes, she uses the actual word "stupid," but also because I refuse to cop to it. The gastric banding failed me or I failed it and according to her, it was stupid of me to have had that surgery. She says it was stupid to spend all that money and go through everything I went through with the gastric banding operations beginning back in 1988. Knowing what I know now, I wouldn't go through that again, would I?

Well, the key phrase is "knowing what I know now." I only know what I know now because I got through what I went through. I wasn't stupid for not knowing. A toddler isn't stupid for falling when they're trying to learn to walk. A scientist isn't stupid for trying a certain combination of chemicals to form a potentially lifesaving drug. It's called "learning."

Being one of the first recipients of the adjustable gastric band back in 1988 as part of Dr. Kuzmak's test group to gain FDA approval for that particular weight-loss surgery device was pretty brave on my part. It was new. There were no ten-year-out success stories, but I didn't care. I was desperate. I had hit my all-time high of two hundred pounds when I first moved out of my parents' house and then gained another hundred pounds in a year's time, bringing me to three hundred pounds. Looking back, I see a number of factors that contributed to this drastic and quick weight gain: I moved out of my parents' house. I was now in full control of what I put into my mouth. No mother-imposed diets, no "Who ate all the____?" from my father. Out on my own in my own apartment, I ate like a kid whose parents are away for the weekend, only now they were away for good. It didn't help that I was moonlighting at a movie theater behind the popcorn stand. It didn't help that movie-theater popcorn slathered in fake butter was one of my favorite foods in the whole world. It didn't help that I could eat buckets of it and never get tired of the taste. The unlimited candy supply didn't help, either.

I was on a too-high dose of a too-strong antidepressant called Imipramine (Tofranil) that caused severe rebound depression, weight gain, and intense adverse side effects upon any attempt at withdrawal.

I was living with an emotionally abusive roommate who resented me for, well, just about everything from my gender to my personality. He shamed me for my appearance, my eating, and my depression.

I hated my day job. I quit, then fell into extreme depression as I scrambled from part-time job to off-the-books jobs to pay the rent.

I binge ate till I passed out more than once a day.

My abusive roommate resented my self-destructive behavior and berated me for it. I remember standing at the refrigerator, asking him if he was going to eat a certain container of leftovers. He threw me a dirty look and said, "Go ahead," then under his breath, "Don't choke on it." I ate it anyway.

Yet for all the self-destructive addictive behavior, part of me wanted to save myself. I knew I had a problem, and I tried to help myself. I recognized that my binge eating disorder involved feeling sick, full, and incapacitated. My research on weight-loss surgeries—and when I say "research," I mean pre-Internet research where I went to the library and looked it up on microfilm and microfiche, in newspapers, journals, books, magazines, and so on—gave me hope that there was a way to stop the weight gain from overeating.

The gastric banding made me think I could circumvent the damage from my binge eating disorder. The operation created a small pouch above the rest of the stomach. This pouch would fill up quickly with very little food and the patient is supposed to feel "full" and "satisfied" the same way one feels when one's stomach is full under normal circumstances. This seemed to be the heaven-sent answer for me. I could trick myself out of this expanding spiral of weight gain by continuing to provide myself with an overly full feeling on a tenth of the amount of food. I aggressively pursued the surgery.

I had no health insurance, so my mother paid the surgeon's fee. I arranged charity care for the hospital. My father scowled and detached from the entire process, saying what I was doing was unnatural and all I needed was some willpower.

This surgery involved a full, open incision, not laparoscopy. The scar looks like the surgeon gutted me from stem to stern, like a fish. The incision was a full twelve inches long. (I just pulled out a ruler and measured the railroad-track scar on my torso.) Healing was painful. They kept me in the hospital for ten days post-op, because my lungs wouldn't clear up. I ran a low-grade fever for days. The nurses were unkind. They scolded me for not wanting to get up out of bed. They scolded me for the condition of my lungs. They scolded me for keeping baby food in a drawer next to my bed. The pureed chicken they tried to feed me made me sick just to smell it. They had no sympathy. I disliked myself and they obliged by disliking me too.

My surgeon didn't have sympathy with the way the pureed chicken made me sick just to smell it. He said he knew I had sneaked in food from the outside. I protested that I wasn't trying to sneak anything, that the hospital food was disgusting and I was hungry. What was the difference if I ate pureed fruit from a jar or pureed crap off my hospital tray? Wasn't all pureed, baby-food consistency stuff created equal? He told me I was trying to cheat the surgery.

It didn't seem to matter to anyone that I couldn't hold down any food at all, whether it was my contraband baby food or the putrid hospital meat. I threw up everything I tried to eat. The surgeon seemed happy that I was puking. As long as I was holding down water, it didn't matter that I couldn't eat.

A few days post-op made me realize that I had been lied to. There was no "full" feeling or satiety. There was only pain, like swallowing a whole peach pit and having it lodge in my esophagus. The peach-pit feeling happened immediately upon ingesting anything, including water. Water, food, anything sat there at the small opening to my stomach, trying to fight its way through the tiny passageway made super-tight by the restrictive band. If I moved around, danced, and burped, eventually liquids and certain soft foods would get past the band. They sent me home from the hospital in that condition.

I ate and puked for a year. I lost one hundred pounds. But—and who doesn't love a big *but*?—the puking did some serious damage to my insides. The band itself was digging into my stomach. The involuntary vomiting caused swelling and irritation that wouldn't abate since I was vomiting multiple times per day. The doctor had to keep loosening the band so that I could drink water and so I wouldn't dehydrate from lack of fluids.

How was this adjustable gastric band tightened and loosened? The band itself was inflatable with saline solution. Imagine a stretchy belt around your waist, an inner tube–style belt that is full of water. If more water is injected inside the belt, the belt gets tighter. Let some water out and the belt gets looser. The gastric band could be tightened or loosened by the injection or withdrawal of saline solution through a reservoir attached by thin tubing to the band itself. The reservoir sat under my skin near my navel. A giant X-ray machine hovered over me as the doc watched a TV screen that directed him where to stick the giant needle that would inject or withdraw the saline.

Over the course of that year, he withdrew the saline several times until the band itself was empty. The daily puking was irritating my stomach lining so bad that it swelled to the point of not allowing even water to pass through. The only hope of loosening the band was to replace it. Eventually, the surgeon had to open me up, through that same twelve-inch incision, and surgically adjust the band. That's when more problems started. He decided that as long as he had me open, he'd replace the old band with a newer model. Bad move.

The newer model failed. It sprang a leak inside me. It couldn't be tightened at all. I was able to eat normally, and I started to gain weight back. No way to fix it without another open surgery. He gutted me again to replace the band entirely. This time, the reservoir flipped over inside me and he couldn't get the needle in to tighten or loosen the band. Again, no way to fix it without surgery.

I threw my hands up. I was tired of the surgeries, tired of the stem-to-stern incisions, tired of the vomiting and restrictive eating. I imagined being free of the band, of being able to eat raw vegetables and salads, whole grains, brown rice, fruit! I decided to try to lose the weight naturally by eating right. I decided to get away from my abusive roommate and move in with my boyfriend.

Another mess. My boyfriend had a bad case of narcissistic personality disorder. He cheated on me relentlessly. He was a demon to live with. He was prone to rages, sullen depressions, and disappearing. He told people I was just his roommate. My eating was out of control again.

The empty band inside me was loose enough to allow most foods to pass through the pouch, so binge eating dangerous amounts of food became my drug of choice once again. The scar tissue from the multiple surgeries caused thick, web-like scar tissue to form inside me, giving me a chronic cough, gastroesophageal reflux disease (GERD), and every once in a while, spontaneous vomiting.

Sure, I could say getting the gastric band was a stupid thing to do, but why would I do that? In hindsight, I would not have done it, but that's hindsight. Having already learned the hard lessons, it's easy to look back and say, "I shouldn't have." I'm where I am now as a product of my mistakes, a product of my hard life lessons, a product of my past.

I'm not stupid, I'm learning. I failed so that I could succeed. Removing the gastric band and converting to a gastric bypass was a difficult surgery because of all the scar tissue and my damaged stomach. It was a rough recovery, painful and feverish.

If only you knew how much it hurts when unsympathetic people say to me, "You brought this on yourself."

June 6, 2007

STAIRS AND THE BONE GRAFT

I'VE BEEN AFRAID OF STAIRS since I was seventeen years old. This is understandable. In August—why is it always *that* month?—of 1981, I was doing something I had no business doing: I was riding a moped. My girlfriend and I each borrowed a moped from our badass almost-biker boyfriends. The boys wanted to ride motorcycles but were underage, so they rode mopeds instead. It was a rare privilege to be trusted with their mopeds for a nice ride around the neighborhood. I had never ridden one before except as a passenger holding onto the waist of the driver. Riding on the back of one of these scooters that sounded like a lawnmower was the most I could do (and even then, I wasn't a good passenger).

Back then, I wasn't even good at riding my bicycle. I did have a bicycle that I rode side-by-side with my tomboy girlfriend, but I could never really keep up with her. I crashed into hedges, fell, couldn't make corners, and walked the damned things down hills because I was afraid to go too fast. I never got the hang of leaning with the bike when making a turn. I steered it like it was a car. Turning the handlebars like a steering wheel didn't make for a tight enough turn, so I crashed into fences and lawns and bushes and anything else the suburbs had to offer at the edges of people's properties.

A moped operates on the same principle. It's not enough to simply steer it around corners. One must lean with the little two-wheel death machine. I didn't lean. I didn't know how. I was going downhill and turning a corner when I crashed into the back of a parked car. I flew through the air over the roof of the car, landed on the hood, and began screaming. My left leg was dangling from the shin down. I had broken the lower third of my tibia clean through. The pain was unreal. The world turned a bright white. I remember screaming, "*Help me!*" over and over. The perfectly mowed lawns of the little Cape Cod houses filled with people. A kind man, a former boxing trainer, came over to me and rubbed my sagging leg. He comforted me as only a veteran could with his expertise from years and years of dealing with broken bones and blood. His pep talk sustained me until the ambulance came. My face was bloody, too.

The EMTs arrived and packed my leg in ice. The pain was unimaginable. I don't know how I didn't pass out. I begged for painkillers but didn't get any for almost two hours. Mercifully, they knocked me out with sodium pentothal so the orthopedist could set my leg. My three main concerns during this emergency-room ordeal were getting relief from the searing pain, how I had ruined my boyfriend's moped, and the trouble I was going to be in with my mother. Narcissist that she is, this was an opportunity to use my hospital stay for attention, to obligate and guilt members of the family regarding how much attention they paid to me (really, her), and to shame me for everything from borrowing the moped in the first place to being nauseated by the pain meds. "It's all that throwing up you've been doing," she'd say when I complained of the dizzying nausea I was suffering as I lay in the hospital bed.

I had a non-union fracture. When the lower third of the tibia is broken completely, it tends to heal reluctantly, if at all. My broken nose, cracked pelvis, broken fibula, and multiple contusions healed in the normal amount of time. One year after the accident, when no bone was forming between the broken pieces of my tibia, the surgeon operated. He grafted tiny bone pieces chipped from my left hip onto the tibia and secured it with a plate and six screws that are in there to this day. It wasn't until two years after the bone graft surgery that the cast came off for good. That's three years in a cast and on crutches.

I missed my senior year in high school. The orthopedist wanted me tutored at home, because my injury was too fragile. I was happy about missing school but not happy about missing concert choir. I had been elected president that year. I managed from home. I graduated from high school with honors. Clifton High had close to nine hundred graduates the summer of 1982. I couldn't walk out onto the football field with my classmates. I was sent out ahead of time on my crutches to sit in the front row. My parents told me that plenty of tissues blotted plenty of eyes when I hobbled up to the microphone on my crutches to sing "The Star Spangled Banner" with the Clifton High School Mustang Band.

For the three years that I had the cast and crutches, I learned to find elevators by following my nose, along with handicap ramps and entrances. My mother never bothered getting a handicap hang tag because she was "too busy for that shit." I had calluses under my arms from the crutches. I walked plenty of long distances on those sticks.

Understandably, stairs terrified me the way going fast on bikes and mopeds terrified me. That fear of free-falling and crashing was over-whelming. I teetered at the tops of staircases for years, feeling queasy with vertigo, even after the cast was off. Even escalators terrified me.

Maybe that fear of free-falling, of going too fast, is somehow connected to my size and my eating disorder. Food is an anchor. Fat is an anchor. Free-fall prevention.

Come now to just a year or so ago. I still have a plate and six screws in my left leg. Sometimes it still aches. I work on a sprawling university campus. As I became heavier and heavier, walking became more difficult. I can tell you where the elevators are in every building on campus. Even before I peaked at four hundred plus pounds, my left leg ached from carrying too much extra weight. My injury from twenty-two years ago hurt from the pounding and pressure of my enormous frame. Stairs made it hurt double. Now to a few months ago. I was with my motivational-speaker friend, Darren, and a few of my students on the second floor of University Hall. We were going to take the elevator down to the first floor, out of consideration for me. Remember, I had just returned to school after a difficult surgery. I had trouble breathing and walking. I weighed over 370 pounds the day of the gastric bypass and it was merely weeks later. Darren had the audacity to ask how much weight I would need to lose before I would start taking the stairs. I told him seventy-five pounds. "How about fifty?" he countered.

It's been months since I returned to school. I've been exercising. I'm feeling lighter and more mobile. Thank God for Darren and his audacity. I was stuck in the habit of using the elevator. I assumed I was still too fat to take the stairs, up or down. He had made me think. He broke the pattern of elevator use with his question. I began to question my assumption about my ability to use the stairs.

Yesterday, Darren and I were on the fourth floor of University Hall. We were talking as we approached the stairs. Rather than make a big deal of it, I just continued our conversation and began descending the stairs in a casual manner, the same way most people do. We chatted and walked down the stairs to the lobby, all four flights. It wasn't until we reached the bottom that he remarked, "You're not even out of breath." It was not that huge of an effort. Walking down the stairs didn't exhaust me, didn't make my leg ache, didn't hurt my knees.

My elevator habit is not a habit any longer. Old habits die hard, but they *do* die . . . if you kill them.

June 8, 2007

Hungry Again

I CRIED A LITTLE THIS morning. I woke up hungry. I looked forward to my nice hot mug of coffee and my superfoods breakfast: whole-grain protein bread with some lean turkey, fat-free cheese, and spicy mustard. Yum! But one serving was all I could eat. One slice of bread. Two slices of turkey. One slice of fat-free cheese. And I was full. Physically full. Emotionally? Not so full.

I wanted at least three more of what I had just eaten. I wanted to feel overly full and deadened. I wanted to numb myself and go back to bed. That option was yanked away from me, like a pacifier from a toddler's mouth. No more overstuffing. No more going numb first thing in the morning. No more getting my blood sugar so high that I pass out, coma- like, on the sofa while the morning talk shows blab me to sleep.

What made me cry? Nothing acute. Nothing specific. I'm just not looking forward to anything in my day today. Going to the gym is not terribly dreadful. I kinda enjoy being there, listening to my homemade mix CDs, perspiring, working out my anger. Shopping with my mother, though annoying at the level of my very soul, is not a God-awful task. It feels good to be able to walk without pain, load and unload the groceries from her car, eat a nice healthful lunch.

Nothing is terribly daunting about my upcoming day, *but* nothing is terribly exciting either. Nothing glitters. Nothing pulses with manic attraction. Nothing much to be passionate about. No keys to jangle in my face to distract me from the pain of the ordinary.

So, I cried. I ate gently, healthfully, carefully, and then just sat here in a state of mild despair. There is nothing to be afraid of, nothing I can put my finger on, yet I'm filled with dread.

Sometimes, it takes a special kind of bravery, a warrior's portion, to face the ordinariness of an ordinary day.

Want to see how I'm doing and receive some free tools for your own success?

Visit LisaSargese.com

June 9, 2007

Fat Towel

I'M THROWING OUT THE TOWEL. It used to be my favorite towel, but not because it was pretty. The colors didn't really match my aesthetic. It's a faded gray with some muted rainbow stripes, nothing like the deep burgundies, golds, and exotic sunset colors of my apartment. It wasn't a designer towel. It wasn't particularly well made, not thick or especially soft, but it was huge.

For years, it was the only towel big enough for me to wrap all the way around me when I emerged from the shower. It was the towel I used when I had company. If I needed to shower and make the mad post-shower dash to my bedroom, passing through the peripheral vision of my living room guests, I used that towel. Not only did it wrap around me, it wrapped around me enough so that I could tuck it in and keep it securely on my body.

At one time, it must have been a giant beach towel. In a previous towel incarnation, it may have served as a blanket on the sand large enough for two people to sit upon. That towel actually traveled with me. If I spent any overnights away from home, I had my favorite towel with me. Chances were that I would have to wrap it around me and sit at the edge of a bed somewhere to do my makeup while others milled about the room. That towel was my robe.

Gradually, over the course of the past year, other towels have begun to fit. Bath towels, towels meant to wrap around a person's body, have begun to do just that. They wrap around me, tuck in neatly and stay on me as I walk from the bathroom to the bedroom. This amazes me.

The shrinking is evident. I'm fitting into the world differently. Yesterday, as I emerged from the shower, it was the old towel's turn to be taken out of the linen closet for its roomy wrap around me. It wraps around me like a gown now.

Then a funny thing happened when I sat down on the edge of my bed to begin my skin-care ritual. I felt the towel rip. It was worn out, thread- bare and coughing its last towel breath. Old faithful favorite had hung in there for me till I no longer needed it. It was old and tired. Time to retire to the rag bin.

I felt like I had reached an important milestone. If that towel had ripped and died on me a year ago, I might have actually cried. It was such a comfort to be able to wrap a clean towel around me after a steamy shower. The other towels were too small. I'd wrap them almost around me then have to hold the two ends as I walked to the bedroom. On chilly mornings, those other towels left me exposed, unwrapped and cold. Old faithful favorite was reliable. Even if I had used it once or twice, I would leave it draped over the chair in my bedroom just in case—just in case there was a chilly morning and I needed the embrace of a towel that actually fit me. Now I have a closet full of towels—plush, fluffy, deep, soft towels that wrap, tuck, and stay.

Old faithful favorite served me well. Ripped and ready to retire, I said goodbye to it and to that part of my life. I shed it the way a butterfly sheds its cocoon. I struggled, fought, and won my freedom. Dried up and no longer useful, it falls away into the wind to get reabsorbed into nature.

June 14, 2007

Good Daughter

I'M TAKING MY EIGHTY-FOUR-YEAR-OLD MOTHER to the beach. I announced this to my friends last night as we sat together sipping coffee. I complained that I knew I would be annoyed for most of the day today. They asked why I was doing it. Before I could answer, a senior mentor of mine said, with no shortage of irony in her voice, "Because she's a good daughter."

We compared notes on our difficult mothers. We decided that our mothers resented us. Rather than revel in their daughters' accomplishments, they felt threatened and tried to cut us down or, worse yet, compete with us. The competitive behavior became worse when a male was involved. It didn't matter if the male was a friend or a romantic interest. They vied for their attention. The analysis helped to put things in perspective. If I think that I'm taking an eighty-six-year-old child to the beach, it won't hurt so much when she acts out.

The perspective helped. Today at the beach, we had a great time. My mother and I spent the day laughing our heads off at the absurdity of being on the beach on such a cloudy, drizzly, cold day. Hardly anything was open on the boardwalk. Even the public bathrooms were closed. When nature called and I bravely waded into the surf I was asked to leave the water by hot-beach-patrol-on-a-dune-buggy-guy. I think he called me "ma'am." He asked me not to even touch the water with my toe, because there were no lifeguards on duty.

This made my mother and me laugh even more. Even the lifeguards were smart enough not to venture onto the beach on a rotten day like today. I put on my jacket and covered my legs with a towel.

"That's good. It'll protect you from sunburn!" my mother joked.

"I better put my sunglasses on, Ma, or the sun will sear my retinas!"

"Lis! Are those seagulls or penguins?" We just got sillier and sillier.

Seeing no breaks in the clouds, we gave up and went for an early lunch. Lobster. Blessed lobster. I haven't had a good piece of lobster in years. The tails have been tough or tasteless. Unless you're in the Ironbound section of Newark or up at Cape Cod, it's not an easy delicacy to find. Since the surgery I wasn't sure I could even tolerate lobster meat.

Today, I ate slowly, methodically, and enjoyed every bite. The lobster was perfect. Even without a drop of drawn butter, the lobster meat had a buttery flavor, a flavor I was never able to notice or appreciate in the past. When I pushed myself away from the table, I felt satisfied. Not overstuffed. Not numb. Not overfull. Not dizzy with too many carbs. Just plain satisfied. Did I crave something sweet for dessert? Yes. We got back in the car and I ate a few small pieces of dried pineapple. Again, I was satisfied.

Mother was well behaved. I ate gently and healthfully. I'm home in time to blog. As soon as I finish here, I'll head over to the gym. All's right with the world, yes? So, why am I sitting here crying my eyes out?

June 15, 2007

Ever Elusive Bikini-Girl Attention

You'll complete me right?
Then my life can finally begin.
I'll be worthy right?
Only when you realize the gem I am."

—Alanis Morissette, "Precious Illusions"

A THICKET OF DARK CLOUDS and the occasional sprinkle made our visit to the beach chilly and unpleasant, but Mom and I made the best of it. We laughed and made our own fun.

The only other people on the beach with us yesterday were some teenage girls who alternated between romping in the foamy surf in their bikinis and snuggling under sweatshirts and towels, huddling together on their beach blanket to keep warm. I guessed they were hungover. Why else would they strip down to their scanty two-piece swimsuits to play in the water on such a cold day? Could it be that they were simply young and carefree? I inferred that they still had enough alcohol in their systems from partying last night at Jenks to keep them from feeling the cold.

I watched them from about fifteen yards away. They had taut little figures. Nothing wobbling except the parts that "should." No extra fat to jiggle and draw attention to itself or induce a toxic flood of shame and discomfort. These girls were firm and shapely. Their long hair whipped around in the wind, thick and glorious. Watching them made me want to look back fondly at my own glory days. I wanted their hard-bodied, carefree romping to remind me of my own teenage days as a bikini girl, but I never had those days. I was never them.

I was once a teenager on the beach but not a hard-body bikini girl. I don't remember ever owning a bikini. At fourteen years old, I was a size twelve. At age sixteen, I was a size fourteen. At eighteen, I was nudging up to a size sixteen. By the time I was twenty-one, I was officially wearing clothes that had "X" on the label. By twenty-three, I was a full-fledged fatty shopping at 16Plus and Lane Bryant.

Of course, these are just numbers, right? Does a person's body make them any more or less entitled to enjoy a day at the beach? Should my level of confidence be tied to the size tag on my plus-size tankini swimsuit? No. Of course not.

As my mother and I sat there shivering and laughing on the cold beach, a dune buggy approached. "Beach Patrol" guys were driving around the beach doing . . . well, patrolling, I guess.

An older guy with salt and pepper hair, probably in his early fifties, and some young dude in the passenger's seat pulled up to the bikini girls who, at that time, were huddling together for warmth under layers of towels and sweat shirts. I could hear the older Beach Patrol guy say to them that they could go to the movies if they wanted to, that there were matinees playing during the day. The girls murmured something polite and the two patrollers drove on in the general direction of my mother and me, though they never came close to us.

In fact, they didn't even look our way. The older guy looked straight ahead and avoided making eye contact with me or my mother. The younger guy hid behind his sunglasses as they drove off without even a nod at us. It wouldn't have been so odd had there been anyone else on the beach. The gaggle of girls and my mother and I were the only ones here. I guess my mother and I didn't rate. We weren't worth greeting. We didn't need checking-up on. We didn't exist.

A few minutes later, the patrollers returned. Again they drove over to the bikini girls, who were still huddling. The salt and pepper guy said he heard good news, that the sun would definitely be out but not until tomorrow. He tried to laugh amiably at his own lame attempt at humor. The girls nodded and made faces like they were being forced to smell something unpleasant. The patrollers drove off again. Again, no acknowledgement of Mother and me.

My mother dozed under her kerchief, oblivious. I felt overlooked. And here I had been feeling so brave. I was actually wearing a swimsuit in public. I was able to walk, to carry things, to set up the beach blanket, to walk to the water and wade for a bit. Last year at this time I was struggling, hardly able to walk or breathe. This year I felt so much lighter, freer. And yet as far as I've come, as hard as I've worked, I was stretched out on my beach blanket, feeling dejected, rejected, and completely invisible. A nonperson.

Back in my teenage days, I was mostly invisible. I was the fat friend to my skinny, well-built girlfriends. Boys who flirted with them on the beach or boardwalk gave me an up-and-down glance and then ignored me like I wasn't even there. They dismissed me. I was thrown back like the unwanted boot caught on a fisherman's line. I didn't rate. I wasn't worth talking to.

Those dune buggy assholes brought back memories of those inglorious teenage times. Please don't try to console me by telling me those Beach Patrol assholes were not worth my getting upset over. I *know* that. Knowing that doesn't make it any easier to be ignored. Jerks or not, they ignored me. I felt worse than unworthy. I felt disgusting.

Did they deem my mother too old to matter and I was what? Just too yucky? Old? Flabby?

God knows how I registered or failed to register in the minds of those Beach Patrollers. I was the pickled beets on the salad bar, a fresh, nutritious food choice trying to compete with the alluring goodness of croutons, macaroni salad, and other more enticing fare. I was purple and pickled. The bikini girls were tasty and seductive. The buggy guys didn't want something with value and inherent goodness. They wanted the obvious, the popular, the immediately pleasurable. Even though I was more nutritious, I wasn't even worth tasting. I didn't even make it onto the plate.

At least that's how I perceived it. Those poor girls must have laughed under their breath both times the beach dicks drove away. I could almost hear them saying, "Yeah right, you old bastard" or, "As if!" and then going on to talk about their latest romantic escapades with Joe Frisbee and Jack Jenks.

OK, so what? I'm invisible now, and there's safety in that. Soon, within the year, it will start to happen. I'll start pinging on the radar. I won't be the fat girl with the pretty face, the pickled beets. I'll be pretty. I'll be the tasty, alluring, more popular choice.

Then what? Then the attention will annoy and offend me. It won't register as sincere. I'll wonder where these men were when I was struggling to rebuild myself. I'll wonder why they didn't notice me when I was painstakingly forming my character and trying so damned hard to be a good person, to be a woman of integrity and compassion. I'll wonder why firm abs and a boob job suddenly make me a worthy dinner companion when, for years, I sat home alone on date nights wondering why I didn't have a boyfriend or anyone to take me away for the weekend.

Please don't try to console me by telling me what wonderful friends I have. I know I have wonderful friends. It is consoling to have wonderful friends. I could pick up the phone right now and arrange a night at a fancy Montclair bistro or a movie or some interesting shopping excursion. I'm grateful. I am. Dates are different than outings with friends. I'm forty- two, and I can't remember the last time I've been kissed, dated, had a real boyfriend. Actually, I can. It was ten years ago. And some boyfriend that was. He cheated on me nonstop.

I bet those bikini girls have plenty of self-esteem issues. I know life isn't perfect for them. Or maybe they do have healthy self-esteem. I don't know. Healthy self-esteem or not, they still ping on the radar. They still get attention. They're witnessed. They're validated. They exist.

June 28, 2007

Isolated Addict

Back in my heavy-eating days, I used to prefer either (a) being with other heavy eaters or (b) being alone so I could eat.

I would look forward to social occasions that involved eating. Movie theaters weren't places to watch movies, they were places to eat heavily buttered (oiled, really) popcorn with peanut M&M's thrown in (thrown in directly on top of the heavily oiled popcorn) and be entertained by a movie while I was eating myself sick.

The carnival wasn't a weird, degenerate place filled with rides and oddities, it was an excuse to eat greasy, fried foods with sideshows to kill time between the food kiosks. Parties? Chips, dip, and finger foods. Shopping? The food court. Restaurants? Pretending to be conversational between bread and butter and too much food. Bars? Popcorn, peanuts, pretzels, and hopefully the diner afterward. The beach? Boardwalk food. Writing a paper at the computer? A dozen Slim Jims. All-you-can-eat buffets? Four giant platefuls plus multiple desserts. Hanging out with friends? Order in and eat till I passed out. A reason to get out of bed in the morning? McDonald's breakfast.

Overeating was a hell of an addiction. Overeating took up most of my time. It wasn't just the eating that consumed time, it was the secretive buying of the food, falling over from the painful feeling of having eaten too much, the digesting, the sugar coma, the passing out and recovery.

If I was out with people, I couldn't wait to get back to my car so I could get to the nearest drive-thru to over order a value-meal binge. If I had company, I couldn't wait for them to leave so I could finish off the rest of our takeout food. Evenings? I remember shopping at the convenience store, buying chips, grabbing Entenmann's cakes, Hostess Twinkies, Drake's Devil Dogs, and ice cream. I'd also buy half-and-half and Sweet'N Low or something to make it look like I was shopping for company. I'd rip open the boxes and eat with my fingers on the way home in the car. Sometimes the food wouldn't make it home. I'd finish off the booty while sitting in the driver's seat, parked in front of my apartment.

Eating was *who I was*. That is, if Aristotle was right when he said, "We are what we do." If we are what we eat, then I was fried, sugary dough covered in melted cheese. I remember the detox. I remember how it felt to abstain from overeating for those first three months following the gastric bypass. I jonesed, bad. I wanted to eat, but I couldn't. So I shivered. I cried. I felt the meaninglessness, the lack of hope, the lack of interest in life. Without my overeating, I felt dead. Life was no fun. I had no reason to get out of bed. No way to reward myself, no way to escape.

It's almost a year later. I overate this morning. I had a few too many bites of leftover (homemade, fat-free) vegetables and curry. I guess I ate about one and a half to two cups of it. That's a lot for my tiny stomach. It hurt. My stomach hurt. I got fever chills (they call it dumping syndrome when too much food enters the lower intestines too quickly). I had to lie down on the sofa for half an hour to get back to feeling normal.

I'm still an addict, but I'm better than I was. Rather than wish my friends would leave so I can eat, I enjoy their company until I pass out from being tired rather than overly full. I enjoy shopping for the actual shopping. All-you-can-eat buffets are more of a chore to find things that I can digest rather than a reason to stuff myself sick. I haven't been to a fast-food drive-thru in months.

The meaninglessness isn't so bad. I get satisfaction from teaching, blogging, and exercising. If I feel binge-y, I eat healthy foods, but overeating is still overeating. Then I suffer the pain and nausea. I'm reminded that bingeing is no longer satisfying. I get over it. I do something productive or go take a nap.

No, I'm not cured, but I'm not killing myself anymore. *But,* I'm still cautiously isolated. I haven't expanded my social life all that much. I'm not out and about the way I could be. I don't look through the *Montclair Times* for free or cheap cultural events and activities. I don't fill my calendar with fun things to do . . . yet.

I'm struggling to enjoy the mundane. There is great satisfaction to be had from doing small chores and accomplishing little tasks. Sometimes I forget. Sometimes I have to remind myself how great I feel after listing a bunch of stuff on eBay or catching up on my filing or doing laundry. Sometimes I have to force myself to get out of the house to remind myself that it feels *good* to be social and to have fun.

Old habits die hard, I guess.

I'm killing the old habits. Little by little, I'm killing the old, self-destructive habits. Little by little I'm learning to love life, even the mundane details, without the allure of passing out from too much food.

June 30, 2007

INTERVIEW QUESTIONS

A BRILLIANT STUDENT FROM NORTHWESTERN University is writing her master's thesis on eating disorders. She asked me to answer the following questions. I'll answer them here on my blog in case the answers are helpful to my readers.

When did you start binge eating?

When I was around five years old. I was a "sneak eater." When my mother wasn't watching me, I'd stuff myself till I was sick on whatever food I could get my hands on.

What, to you, is a binge as opposed to overeating?

Overeating is any eating over the prescribed limits of whatever the portion size is supposed to be. A giant bowl of cereal three times the recommended serving size could be overeating and not a binge. A binge is characterized by lack of enjoyment or lack of awareness of what one is shoving into one's mouth or eating till one is physically uncomfortable.

What do you typically binge on?

Anything. Whatever is on hand. Everything from room temperature SpaghettiOs direct from the can to pizza to ice cream to mayonnaise on bread.

When and why?

Usually at night. Why? To go numb. To distract myself from how unhappy I am. To avoid feeling my feelings. To push down the angry words that should have come out of my mouth during the day.

How do you feel right before a binge and after?

Before a binge, I feel confused, sad, tired, lonely, angry, anxious, hungry, and desperate. After the binge I feel dead, tired, exhausted, numb, sick, regretful, and dizzy.

What methods have you taken to attempt to stop bingeing?

I blog every day as a way to sort through, confront, and actually *feel* my feelings rather than avoid them or stuff them down with food. I had a gastric bypass as a catalyst to begin eating less junk and eating more high- quality foods. I exercise six days a week to help vent my emotions and diffuse my anxiety and to get strong. I was in therapy for twenty years or so.

Which of these have been the most successful?

Every one of the above were necessary, except the bypass. The bypass was my chosen catalyst to begin a life of wellness. Any catalyst will work. Therapy, support group, eating well, and exercising are essential. No exceptions.

Do you feel like gastric bypass surgery helped with your binge eating, or did you need to address the disorder separately from the surgery?

The surgery helped but was not the only thing that helped. Binge eating was a way of life for me. I had to make a *new* way of life, a complete lifestyle change. Transformation. New eating habits. New emotional outlets. New integrity. Honesty. Will. Determination.

July 12, 2007

SCRITCH, SCRITCH, SCRITCH

WHY CAN'T I JUST HAVE a back rub?

If given a choice between movie-theater popcorn or a nice scritch, scritch, scritch up the back of my neck? Scritch me, baby, please. I love getting massaged. I get all mushy inside just watching someone else get a massage. I don't think I get touched enough.

I shared this revelation with my fellow hypnotists last night at our chapter meeting. I expected head-nodding and validation. I expected someone to reach into their bag for a coupon for a massage. I half expected one of them to offer me a little back rub. Nope. The closest I came to getting that was a referral to try Massage Envy in Cedar Grove. Hey, great referral. I will check it out.

More disturbing was the way they deflected my needs and shamed me. I got a downpour of suggestions of how to get my back rub fix some other way. One woman suggested that I "give more of myself" and find pleasure in doing some sort of work for others. She said that I should volunteer with children because giving to the little folk can be so satisfying.

Someone asked if I had any pets and suggested I volunteer at an animal shelter.

Someone suggested that I exercise.

One of the brightest and most credentialed people in the room suggested that what I really needed was nurturing and the full attention of a loving partner. Then she qualified what she said by adding that she wanted that for herself and may be filtering her comment through her own needs. That made sense. She admitted that she was speaking more about herself rather than what I had expressed. That's why she's one of the smartest people in the room. That was very accountable of her to wonder if she was projecting her needs on to me. And then again, she could be right about what I need.

I think I ended the discussion with, "I really just want a nice back rub."

How strange. How strange that the immediate reaction to my expressing my need for physical attention would be to suggest things other than filling that specific need. This was a room full of healing professionals. Didn't they understand what I was asking for? It was hard enough to dissect my feelings and come up with a need that I was brave enough to express. How did they take me from the massage table to volunteering for an after-school reading program? I felt as if I had suggested something objectionable, immoral, improbable, and inappropriate.

No wonder we're such a low-touch, isolated culture of individuals. Being touched is a salable service billable by the hour, not something nice we can just ask for from a friend—not something to get or give freely.

I remember the one and only time I paid for a professional massage. I had a migraine, my one and only migraine headache, that lasted for days. My chiropractor, my osteopath, and my acupuncturist couldn't help me get rid of it. I was in blinding pain. The pain killers and anti-inflammatory drugs were barely making a dent in my suffering. In my desperation, I called a professional masseur.

He came to my apartment with his massage table. He seemed a bit nervous about my size and the table's weight limit (I was about four hundred pounds at the time). I told him about my headache. He said he wasn't sure he could help me, but he'd try. I hoisted myself up onto the table and lay face down. He poured almond oil on me and began. It felt *great.* I sighed a bit in appreciation. A few minutes into the massage, he said, "I'm not sure what I'm supposed to be doing here." *Huh?* I told him he was doing fine. He seemed perplexed. I wasn't sure why.

Was it my size? Did my large body confuse him? I was too intimidated to ask.

He gave me the hour massage. My headache was gone for good. He had cured me. I tried to tell him how much better I felt. He stammered and burbled about being unsure he had done me any good. I asked about seeing him another time. He told me he was busy and didn't usually make house calls. I told him I'd come to his office. He didn't seem happy about that suggestion.

I never called him. Although his massage had released my tension and cured my headache, his demeanor made me uncomfortable. Till this day I'm not sure if I was being paranoid or if he was fat-phobic. Some folks just don't like fat people, I guess.

Do you have to wonder why I'm ashamed to go and seek out any kind of professional help that involves being touched by another person? The guy helped me but made me feel like a freakish monster in the process. I ask a room full of hypno-counselors what to do about not being touched enough and they imply that I'm being selfish.

No wonder I blog. I don't have to see anyone's disapproving looks or risk being shamed for expressing my needs. I still wish someone would just scratch my back—for free.

July 13, 2007
MY ATKINS PROBLEM

BACK BEFORE THE GASTRIC BYPASS, I was able to eat large quantities of food. I still had the failed gastric band inside me, but food could pass through it fairly easily. I was large and gaining, so I was always trying to balance my need for food with a way to take off weight. People told me to try the Atkins diet because it allows you to eat lots of protein, which they promised would make me feel less hungry. Of course the Atkins diet works, if by "works" you mean that people lose weight from following it.

But—and it's a big bad *but*—do they keep the weight off?

If you're like me, you didn't read the Atkins diet books thoroughly. If you're like me, you were selective about the advice you absorbed from them. I chose to hear, "Eat all the fatty protein you want. Don't bother with portion control or calorie counting. Eat meat and cheese to your heart's content. You're like an Eskimo. You'll store the fat you need for winter. Fat is good. Eat fat. Cheese is your friend. Bacon is your buddy. Eat, eat, eat, eat, eat . . . " That's not what the Atkins diet advises, but that's what I heard. I heard it telling me to eat.

So, I did. I ate. All my life I've heard, "You're too fat. Stop eating!" Hearing any message that allowed me to feed myself was a welcome relief. At four hundred plus pounds, I ate. I could hardly move. Merely standing made me out of breath. Grocery shopping was painful and mostly out of the question. (Thank God for my dear friends Matt and Marni, who grocery shopped for me when I was incapacitated.)

I fed myself at the drive-thru, because I couldn't stand at the stove to cook. McDonald's breakfast was my reason to get out of bed in the morning. With my Atkins mentality, I could stuff myself sick on sausage patties, scrambled eggs, cheese, and the innards of McMuffins, with their disk-shaped egg pucks covered with plastic-orange cheese. I was never happier than when McDonald's offered its Steak, Egg, and Cheese Bagel sandwich. I'd eat everything except the bagel part. And then I was diagnosed with type 2 diabetes.

The doctors cited my weight as the cause. They didn't ask what I was eating. The doctors told me to go on a weight-loss diet. The doctors sent me to dietitians, who showed me toy food to demonstrate portion control. I was given stacks of literature about diabetic portions and food selections. It wasn't enough food for me. I was always hungry.

When I spent three weeks in the hospital with the killer boils and carbuncles from a staph infection so lethal it took round-the-clock intravenous antibiotics to cure me, I sat in bed starving. Not because they didn't feed me. They fed me. They fed me three meals and two snacks according to the American Dietetic Association's diabetes-control menu. The hunger was agonizing. The amount of food they fed me wasn't enough. I was fidgety between meals. I craved food, any food. I got headaches. I drank tea to try to stave off the hunger. I munched on chewable vitamins and pretended they were candy. I sat in my hospital bed and watched the clock. I listened hopefully for the squeaky wheels of the food cart to come down the hall.

When my meal would finally arrive, I ate everything on my hospital food tray. Everything. Even the garnish. The dishes looked like they had been washed by the time I was done. I would be hungry an hour later. Not "mouth hungry." Not emotionally hungry. Stomach-growling hungry.

I wanted the insides of a Double Whopper with cheese. I wanted Oscar Mayer Bologna with Hellmann's mayonnaise. I wanted a block of cheddar cheese. I wanted my "protein fix." In that sorry state, how could I have stuck to a healthy eating plan? How could I have been satisfied with a normal portion of food? I couldn't see it for myself. I couldn't envision eating less than a giant Eskimo weight lifter's portion of fast-food meats and cheeses.

My stomach wanted heavy food. My stomach wanted greasy meat. My stomach growled like an angry beast when I didn't feed it what it wanted. It truly felt like a monster inside me. I longed to be free. I couldn't tell anyone how hungry I was all the time. If I did, they might call me a glutton. I didn't expect sympathy and understanding. I didn't imagine there was any science behind why I was so hungry all the time. I blamed my stomach.

I had my gastric bypass in August 2006. The freedom I craved is mercifully here. I've been free from the demands of the monster for almost a year now. I am eating impossibly less food than I ever imagined I could live on. I actually *like* lean protein. I fill up on dainty portions of food. I haven't been to a drive-thru in months.

The evidence points to my stomach. It must have been my stomach. It really was to blame after all.

July 18, 2007
USELESS INTERVENTIONS

I WAS OVER FOUR HUNDRED pounds at my heaviest. No intervention in the world could have changed my body, but still, people tried.

My father exploded at me one day. He slammed his palm on the dining room table repeatedly and yelled, "Lose weight, goddamnit! All your problems are because you're too heavy! Lose weight!" He was more than angry—he was enraged. I calmly walked out of the house and didn't start crying till I was alone in my car. Had he motivated me? No. I was humiliated. I felt misunderstood and deeply hurt. I was angry and not at all motivated to change. I wanted sympathy, understanding, and encouragement. He gave me the opposite. He treated me like my size was evidence that I was being stubborn and stupid. I stayed the same weight for six more years.

My family doctor, the general practitioner, told me I was an addict. He told me horror stories about people being confined to bed after a stroke caused by fatness. He told me frightening tales of amputations due to out-of-control diabetes, also caused by fatness. He told me I was killing myself. He said I was an addict and I needed a 12-step program, the last hope and only option for someone like me. Had he motivated me? No. I felt misunderstood and hurt. I was angry and not at all motivated to change. I wanted sympathy, understanding, and encouragement. He gave me the opposite. He talked to me like I was stubborn and stupid. I stayed the same weight for six more years.

No one had to tell me I was killing myself. I knew it. I felt like I was dying every single day. I could hardly move. I didn't walk, I lurched from sofa to bathroom to bed. My breathing was labored. My blood sugar was out of control. I was tired all the time. My life barely mattered to me.

Good thing I believe in karma. A huge part of what motivated me to start getting well was the notion that if I didn't handle these issues in *this* life, I would reincarnate and have to deal with these issues in my next life. I didn't want to go through this pain and suffering again. I was miserable enough in the here and now. The thought of having to suffer again, as a different person, fat, in pain, with people scolding me like I was an errant child, made me want to get this life lesson over with in this incarnation.

Another huge part of what made me want to heal was the kindness and caring staff at the hospital where I spent three weeks on round-the- clock antibiotics for a killer staph infection due to out-of-control diabetes. I was covered in super painful boils and carbuncles. The open sores, giant saucer-size infected craters, had to be cleaned and dressed twice a day by a registered nurse. I received care, hands-on care. One-on-one attention. It was their duty to keep me alive. I mattered.

They encouraged me. They told me what a great job I was doing by taking my showers twice a day. They told me that other patients in this condition, with even fewer boils and carbuncles than I had, didn't comply with doctors' orders. They didn't take their showers (the water burned the open sores and standing in the shower was a feat of remarkable strength for me at four hundred pounds). They were impressed that in my weakened, fevered, painful condition, I forced myself out of bed and into that tepid shower twice a day. Part of me wanted to live.

I complied 100 percent with what felt like a starvation diet they had me on in the hospital for those three weeks. The eighteen-hundred-calorie diet they put me on left me hungry all the time, even an hour after I had just eaten, but because I was compliant, because I didn't sneak any outside foods into my mouth, because I ate what and when they told me to, my blood sugar came under control. When the aides came in to jab my finger with a needle to test my blood sugar, then burn the open wound with an alcohol swab, they would say positive things to me as they read the improved blood sugar level. They gave me a "Good girl!" or "Much better!" or "Keep up the good work!" as they recorded my blood sugar reading in their chart. I felt so validated.

Friendly greetings and banter with the people who mopped my hospital room floor, the folks who delivered my meal tray, the woman selling magazines, the chaplain who prayed with me, the orderlies who wheeled me around, all these kind strangers made me see that there was somthing possible beyond my world of misery. The little compliments, the interactions, the mild praise made me feel better about myself. It showed me that there were people, other than my friends and family, who could and would actually care for me. That was what I craved so bad: care. Not someone to scold me for not taking care of myself, but someone to tell me I was good, worthy, worth saving, worth their time and trouble.

All the scolding in the world wouldn't and didn't help me. That's what burns me up about the professionals on shows like *Big Medicine*. They have that scolding tone, that last-hope attitude. They seem to believe that if their mighty efforts (in this case, via weight-loss surgery) didn't inspire that eight-hundred-pound man to change, then he was utterly hopeless. If he wasn't going to comply with their expert advice, then he must want to die. They have the attitude that says, "If this doesn't wake him up to the fact that he's killing himself, then nothing will. We can't force him to comply with the post-op plan. We gave him the surgery, now the rest is up to him. We've done all we could. If he fails, it's his own fault." Did it every occur to them that their methods were lacking?

Don't they know that force creates resistance? I thought that was a simple, scientific fact about the world. I heard the same thing about myself—that I was defective. I heard that I was hell-bent on destroying myself. I was told that I had a "death wish." I heard that I was an addict.

How was that supposed to help me? Was it true even true? Did these people have any idea the physical and emotional *pain* I was in? Of course it looked like I had a death wish. I wanted to die so the pain would stop.

I wasn't overeating for pleasure. I wasn't overeating out of lack of willpower. I was miserable. I didn't have a sense of self-worth. I didn't want to take care of myself. I didn't care enough about my own life to live it healthfully. When you're like that, like I was, hearing that I was killing myself was simply redundant. I'm killing myself? Yeah, I know. So what? My life was an open grave and I was slowly, handful by handful, spoonful by spoonful, forkful by forkful, pulling the dirt in on top of me. I was burying myself alive. The scare-tactic folks were standing at the edge of my open grave yelling down at me that I was killing myself. It didn't help. What I needed was someone to reach down and give me a hand up. Kindness. Encouragement. Positive reinforcement. Understanding. Sympathy. Empathy.

I'm going to find a way to bottle and sell: Kindness. Encouragement. Positive reinforcement. Understanding. Sympathy. Empathy. Hell, I'll give it away whenever I can afford to. Then maybe some lives will be saved, the way mine was. I don't want anyone to suffer the way I have.

July 19, 2007
SMOKE AND RICE

I MET A WOMAN WHO lost too much weight after her gastric bypass. It was a perfectly sunny Saturday. My mom and I were making our garage sale rounds. We pulled up to a nice suburban home where two women were seated in lawn chairs on the front lawn. The blonde woman smoking a cigarette was older, maybe in her late fifties, and skeletal. The younger woman, her daughter perhaps, was a pretty, heavyset blonde who had to weigh 250 or more by the looks of her.

There were clothes hanging in their garage. I was hopeful. Whenever I pull up to a garage sale that's selling clothes and I see a plus-size woman, I imagine there's a good chance that I'll find some great bargain clothes that will fit me. I browsed through some size eighteens that, by the grace of God, actually fit me! I was elated. The ladies were friendly when I approached them with my pile of clothes. The skinny woman asked if I had taken a look at the nice jackets that were hanging in the garage. I had not. I always imagine the really good things are too small for me. I've been conditioned to believe that nice things, pretty things, are not meant for me to wear. If I try something on, I'm afraid it will not button, zipper, or fit, and I'll have to hang it back up feeling shamed. So no, I had not even considered the jackets. The skinny lady, cigarette dangling from her mouth, brought a gorgeous faux-fur hooded jacket over to me. I reluctantly tried it on. It fit! It fit beautifully, like it had been made for me.

I walked over to the car to show my mother. The skinny woman followed. She told us that the jacket used to be hers but she had a gastric by-pass and lost over two hundred pounds. Everything changed between us. She was no longer a skinny woman to me. She was a former fat woman, someone who understood me.

I told her about my surgery. She told me about hers. She lifted her shirt to show me her excess skin. It was stretchy and wrinkled like thin rubber, but—and this is the big *but* that gave me incredible hope—she didn't have a pannus. She didn't have a hanging abdomen. Her apron of flab was gone. Empty. All that was left was skin.

My dream, goal, plan is to have as few corrective surgeries as possible to reconstruct my deflated body. It looked like that excess skin of hers could be snipped off in one procedure. She had what I wanted, but she was unhappy. She had recently lost her husband after a prolonged illness. During his illness and fading, she didn't eat. All she lived on were coffee and cigarettes. She said she was underweight by forty pounds. She told me she threw up every day.

I noticed she had a half-full mug of undercooked, white rice next to her lawn chair. I didn't make any comment about it. To myself I thought, "What the hell are you doing eating hard, white rice? No wonder you're throwing up!" White rice is sticky. It balls up on its way down the magical road to the small opening that leads to a gastric bypass patient's small intestine.

I thanked her up and down a thousand times for suggesting I try on that beautiful jacket. It was well made, stylish, with thick satin lining and a ridiculous bargain at only ten dollars! I would have had to pay $140 to buy it new.

I pray that she saves her life. I pray that God has mercy on her grieving heart. She was so brave to have lifted her shirt to show me her wrinkly elephant skin. She gave me hope that I'll need very little corrective surgery after I've lost the rest of this weight. She gave me the courage to try something on in hopes that it would fit, and it did. I hope she is able to eat something solid soon before she disappears.

July 30, 2007

ENERGY YET?

I'VE BEEN WAITING FOR THE energy. I've been waiting for the energy that is supposed to come from working out. Ninety percent of the people I talk to about my six-days-a-week exercise schedule respond by saying, "And don't you have more energy now?"

Um, no, not really. I have more energy than before but I use it all up at the gym. Energy-wise, I'm barely breaking even. I don't feel like doing much when I get home. I feel like sprawling out on the sofa when I get home. The most movement I feel like doing is picking up the remote or clicking my mouse.

They say a body in motion tends to stay in motion. I'm not finding that to be true. My vision was to have abundant energy, to be vibrant, awake, alert, and unstoppable. Back in my early twenties, I worked from morning till way past midnight. I'd work at my day job, go right to my night job and pick up any shifts I could get as a cater waiter on weekends. I hustled. I worked seven days a week to keep the roof over my head. I want to have that kind of energy again.

Back then, the energy was a by-product of youth. This time, I hoped it would be the result of hard work, commitment, and vision, but it's not happening yet. I'm tired and draggy.

It's frustrating being so tired when I'm supposed to be more energetic. When does the energy start to happen?

I'm still fighting the good fight! Check out LisaSargese.com to see wear I'm speaking and to find out when the next book is available!

August 5, 2007

GROCERY PEACE

I USED TO PANIC AFTER grocery shopping. Having food in the house made me nervous. I wanted to eat it all at once. Opening the refrigerator and seeing the shelves fully stocked made me anxious. I wanted to stuff it all into my mouth before . . . before what? Before someone could come along and eat it out from under me? Take it away from me? Declare that meal-time was over and shame me for eating past mealtime?

Yesterday, I opened the fridge and the old feelings came back for a brief moment. There was fruit, turkey, milk, tofu, fat-free cheese, two kinds of fat-free pudding, two kinds of yogurt, protein bread, blueberry preserves, sugar-free ice pops, sugar-free chocolate pops. The amount of food was overwhelming. I looked at the bounty in the fridge and felt the old panic. I felt the need to fill my arms with food containers, waddle to the couch, and stuff myself, but I didn't. I did sit on the couch in front of the TV, but I nibbled on some Wasa and then didn't feel like eating much else.

Old habits die hard. Old habits die hard, until you kill them. When I opened the fridge and felt the old panic trying to grip me, I stood there and noticed my feelings. "Eat everything! Eat everything, quick!" my brain shouted. Then a different part of my brain shouted back. "Ewwww, no! I'll be sick to my stomach if I do that. I'll feel nauseated!" My brain volleyed back and forth between those two thoughts. Eventually, I settled on "No, I'll feel nauseated if I overeat," and shut the fridge.

Funny how the brain runs on automatic. Funny how the old habits kick in so easily.

It didn't take *too* much effort to kill the inclination to stuff myself. It did take a bit of effort, though. I used the idea of intestinal distress to talk myself out of the binge. I hate feeling nauseated. Well, everyone hates feeling nauseated, *but* some of us will eat things that nauseate us. Sometimes the momentary pleasure is worth the nausea, or, worse yet, we disassociate from the delayed consequences.

Back in my eating days, a face-stuffing binge always ended in gastric distress: pain, nausea, cramps, indigestion, heartburn. The prospect of nausea didn't stop me back then. I heard about a gastric bypass patient who still suffers terribly from disordered eating. She won't eat until the afternoon. She starves herself all morning until a few hours past lunchtime. By that time, she's famished. Maybe her mini-stomach growls. She goes to a fast-food drive-thru, eats a supersize meal, and suffers. Sometimes she'll make herself throw up to get some relief. Dear God, have mercy. Have mercy on us.

I could call binge eating a disease, but I prefer to call it a behavioral disorder. Calling binge eating a "disease" makes it sound like a sickness that the person has no power over. Calling it a "disease" seems to lead to a victim's mentality, an "I can't help it, I'm sick" way of thinking. At a support group meeting, a young bulimic once spoke that way. She said she understood her behavior as being a symptom of her disease, as if to say she understood that she was sick and bingeing and purging were just parts of it, like sniffling and coughing when you have a cold. She said she could gauge how sick she was by monitoring her symptoms. If she binged and purged often, then her sickness was exacerbated. If she refrained, then she was in a kind of remission.

I don't like that kind of thinking for me. It keeps me removed from my own behavior. It leads to the thinking that our bodies are more powerful than our will. Our bodies influence our will, but no way am I going to agree that a physical addiction is the sole determinant of our behavior. I believe our will has the final say.

I'm not an outsider looking in and saying that addicts are weak-willed. On the contrary, I *am* an addict, and yes, I know what it feels like to jones. I know what it feels like to have a physical need so compelling that my body almost, *almost* runs completely on automatic.

Remember, I had undiagnosed sleep apnea. Sleep deprivation and oxygen deprivation made me so tired and lethargic, I didn't have the strength to give a crap about my own life. I desperately wanted energy. Not knowing what was wrong, I self-soothed with food. Sugary food. Junk food.

I binged for the emotional numbness. I binged because I needed energy. It was a combination of addiction and physical need that drove me to overeat.

During the three months following my gastric bypass surgery, I felt the jones. I trembled. I ached. I suffered the fever chills. There were days, most days, when I didn't even want to go on living. The utter hopelessness of those feelings was barely tolerable. My drug of choice was taken from me.

It was my will, my desire to live, that kept me going. I had faith that "this too shall pass" and that these feelings were only temporary. I was right. The feelings passed. I'm feeling better. Life is kinda fun. There are days when I feel happy. There are times when I feel joy. My will to live is getting stronger.

I'm still an addict. I still have to fight the urge to go numb. I have to force myself to get dressed and socialize. I have to force myself to clean up my apartment to make it welcoming to company. I have to stop myself from overeating. The inclinations are still there. The urge to destroy myself is still there, but it's losing the fight. My will to live is slowly winning.

Even if I never cross the finish line, even if the race is never won once and for all, I'm ahead.

I'm in the lead.

August 7, 2007

Recovered

I'VE LOST 120 POUNDS IN one year's time. It was all fat, no lean muscle mass or water weight, I lost actual fat. I work out for sixty plus minutes per day, six days a week. I don't count calories. I have no idea how many calories I consume in a given day, and I don't care. I eat when I'm hungry. I eat till I'm full. When I'm thirsty, I drink.

Simple. Simple, but hard won—so very, very hard won. I am recovering from a severe binge eating disorder. Severe. Severe as in 3,000–20,000 calories in a given binge. Severe as in three different drive-thru meals in under an hour, plus dessert. Severe as in a giant-size, heavily oiled movie-theater popcorn plus peanut M&M's and SNO-CAPS. I recovered from that.

I was traumatized by my hunger. I'd wake up and avoid eating for as long as I could, because I feared I would overeat and incapacitate myself with too much food. I was afraid that once I started eating, I wouldn't stop.

I think I've discovered the physical cause of binge eating. Dieting is the main cause of binge eating. Starve the body and it will crave any food it can get its hands on, and it will hold onto fat in preparation for anticipated periods of famine (calorie-restricted dieting).

It's a cycle. Hey, don't take my word for it. Do the research. I've done the research over many years and lived it firsthand. You can do the research or take a look at your own life. Have diets worked for you and everyone you know? Has any diet worked in the long-term? Has counting calories worked for you in the long-term? If you've lost weight, did you keep it off for at least five years?

This is what I hear from dieters, "Oh, Lisa. The diets *did* work in the beginning, but I'm weak-willed and went off the diet and now the weight is back. If I had stuck with it, it would have worked in the long-term. It's not the diet's fault, it's my lack of willpower!" I don't think that all of people who diet are lacking willpower when they gain weight back. There must be something else working against them.

I have a lot of damage control to do. I abused my body with binges and dieting (dieting is just another word for "purging") for years. Living on a high-protein, high-fat diet for years and restricting carbs messed up my metabolism. My poor body needs balanced nourishment, bad!

My body is a war zone. I'm covered in battle scars inside and out.

I'm still craving the abundant energy and clear-headed-ness of abundant health that's supposed to come with exercise and weight loss. There are many, many causes for the effects in our lives. Physical causes. Emotional causes. Psychological causes. A conspiracy of causes, a demonic team effort keeps people fat, sick, and sedentary. We can't only address one aspect of our health and expect healing of the whole person.

August 8, 2007

A Whole Year

WE CELEBRATED MY FORTY-THIRD BIRTHDAY tonight at a fabulous Moroccan restaurant. I was surrounded by loved ones in the most luscious, beautiful atmosphere. Balloons were floating, gifts abounded, and the food was just phenomenal. I ate like a queen. No, really, like a queen. It wasn't merely because the food was incredibly expensive. It wasn't just that the food was indescribably delicious. It wasn't only the visually stunning way it was served that made it queenly fare.

It was how I ate it. I've never watched a queen eating, but I imagine it's very daintily. Tiny bites. Slowly and methodically. Not slopping all over the front of her blouse. No gulping. No oinking pig noises. I remember back in my binge-eating days how many pajama tops and T-shirts were ruined with stains from slopping red sauce or grease or chocolate down the front of myself. I remember eating so much so fast I actually made grunting pig noises as I ate, complete with hiccups and burping. Not very queen-like.

The surgery forces me to eat slowly. For the past year, it has forced me to eat slowly, to chew every bite, to pause to see if I'm satiated. And now these slow, methodical necessities are habits.

I was slowly, methodically enjoying my exquisite Moroccan feast. Add to it the wine and the chattiness that comes with it (maybe the chatty wine high was not very queen-like) and I ended up with three to-go containers after my birthday feast. I barely ate.

The bites I did take were tasty explosions of distinct flavors: biting cinnamon; flowery saffron; puckery lemon; cool, sweet yogurt. Each dish tasted like it was lovingly prepared with artful, careful pride, the way a royal chef might cook for a queen. When Linda, our lovely server, poured our after-dinner tea from a silver teapot held three feet above our etched tea snifters, we could all smell the fresh garden mint sprinkling into the air around us. Ah, what a sensual experience.

Food should be like that, always—succulent. I want that for me and my friends. Having nice things for myself and only myself would be no fun. I want my friends there with me, enjoying the finer things.

As a binge-eating food addict, I found it difficult to appreciate life through the food-stuffed, deadened fog I was living in. It was painful to walk around the places I love most (the New Jersey shore; Charleston, South Carolina; campus; any park or flea market in the sunshine; New York City). I could barely cover a two-block distance without having to stop, sit, pant, and rub my aching knees. Once in a while, if I was out with people at a nice restaurant, I could enjoy the succulence of well-prepared food. The need to be socially appropriate kept me from gulping it down. The company helped me to pace myself and enjoy what was in front of me, but someone else always picked up the tab.

As I get stronger, I get the urge, the inclination, the need to be more independent, to pick up the tab for my own lifestyle. I want to own my circumstances. I want to own my life. I am standing. I am standing and not counting the seconds till I can sit down. I am wearing a size eighteen down from a size thirty-two. I blood sugar is under better control. I can breathe more easily.

This next year is about radical healing. Time to repair the damage done by years of steady destruction. Time to heal my self-esteem and gain confidence in my ability to use my passions, my talents, my work to translate into an abundant income to support my dream lifestyle:

eating like a queen with my beloved friends, living in comfort in surroundings paid for and created by me, and satisfaction in knowing I am helping others to do the same. By the way, in eight more days, it will be my one-year gastric bypass anniversary. They call it a "surgiversary."

August 9, 2007
THAT MANOR

LAST NIGHT, MY MOTHER AND I went to a fancy buffet at a famous catering hall in West Orange, New Jersey. It's kinda lovely for a trumped-up wedding factory surrounded by photo-op gardens, gazebos, and manmade fountains. It was once a proud, sprawling, private estate. The beauty of the place is enhanced by its location on manicured grounds and the gorgeous mahogany woodwork inside. What was once a stately manor built close to a century ago is now a catering hall and restaurant where middle-class and working-class folks can play dress-up and pay way too much money for mediocre food.

I remember when I was a little girl, my parents would take me there for special occasions. Being there was a special occasion in itself. Looking up at those chandeliers glitzing on the ceiling made me think of what Cinderella's life must be like living in her castle surrounded by rich-people things. Dressing up for our night out made our impending gorge-fest seem more festive. My father would shave for the second time that day and smelled like fresh aftershave. My mother wore her dangly earrings and heavy eyeliner. We would each order a cocktail. My father had his Manhattan, my mother her ginger ale, and I had my Shirley Temple. My mother pointed out the piped-in elevator music and said that was what dinner music should sound like. She said she didn't like clunky jazz with intermittent caterwauling by some lounge singer that you hear in those other restaurants.

When we went out as a family, my parents were mostly on their best behavior in deference to our expensive night out. They were too busy eating and raving about the fanciness of the whole experience to find fault with each other. Do you have to wonder why I associate food with comfort? We went to the buffet and ate to get our money's worth. We put away a lot of food. My mother, father, and I had very good appetites.

Returning to that same restaurant thirty years later was emotionally significant. I resurrected the cocktail memory by having two strong Bloody Marys. They were exceptionally good, probably the best thing that I had all night. The buffet was visually overwhelming; piles of crusty bread, an embarrassment of shrimp, a dogpile of steamed lobster that disappeared mere minutes after being filled by the harried kitchen staff who dutifully replenished it so no one would have to wait more than thirty seconds to load their plate. It all looked so good. Looks deceived.

The shrimp, though plentiful, did not taste fresh. It tasted weak, wilted, and thawed out.

The lobster was OK, but it didn't inspire me to stuff myself the way my mother did. The whole affair was like an eating contest. People piled their plates with lobster then drowned it in drawn butter and ate with haste so they could get some more, as if someone would tap their watch and kick them out before they could stuff themselves with more than what their dinner bill indicated they had eaten.

I really wanted some of the steamed vegetables. My mother made me feel guilty for wanting to eat something that I could "eat any time" and hinted that eating the seafood would mean I would get our money's worth. I wanted to puke. I heard people comparing their lobster consumption.

"How many did you have? Four? I had six!"

I saw the same people returning to the steamed lobster vat—a stainless steel server, elegant looking but fish-stinky—to get four on their plate. The steamed lobsters were halved, so four equaled two whole lobsters. Since they were cut in half, there was no cracking, breaking, or bib-wearing for the patrons. I managed to eat one. That is, one half of a steamed lobster. That's all I could handle. Eating the six small shrimp filled me up. I had no room for much else.

My mother guilted me into tasting more food. I tried the sea bass. Tasteless. I sampled the cardamom chicken. Tough. I tried to savor the scallops and shrimp Newburg. Utterly without flavor. "This is a sham!" I thought. These folks are under the impression that they're having an elegant dining experience. They think that heaping portions of seafood have something to do with wealth and class. This sham of a fakey dinner buffet is a way to fool working-class folks into thinking they're getting something of quality in exchange for their hard-earned dollars. I didn't know where to direct my anger.

Yearning for satisfaction and wanting to get my mother's money's worth, I prepared myself for some chocolate. Dessert was lovely to look at but undelightful to know. I figured I could take a bite or two of the luscious desserts, like a sampler, and enjoy myself. Not so. The desserts were so rich and so sugary my teeth stung and my throat burned from the onslaught of processed sweetness. I didn't feel the rush of pleasure that I once felt from eating rich cakes, creams, and pastries. The little girl who used to fill her plate with desserts and go up to the buffet for seconds is a relic. The little girl who would stuff herself till she was incapacitated with too much food is a thing of the past forever. I felt nauseated. I wanted to leave.

When I got home, I stretched out on the couch to recover. After a few hours, I was able to eat two orange bell peppers to clean out my system. I felt much better.

August 16, 2007
THE SURGI-VERSARY

A YEAR AGO TODAY, I weighed 377 pounds. I woke up in the intensive care unit of Valley Hospital in Ridgewood, New Jersey, after surgery to remove a twenty-year-old, failed gastric band and revise it to a medial RNY gastric bypass. The operation took five and a half hours. My surgeon had to maneuver around adhesions, scar tissue, and my fatty liver in order to make the operation a success.

The surgical team kept me alive despite my blood sugar climbing to a dangerous level during the surgery. Because of my out-of-control diabetes, my healing was impeded. A painful "collection"—a hematoma—formed inside me where my stomach was divided. My red blood cells crapped out on me. They had to pump two bags of someone else's blood into me to keep me afloat. I spent a total of twelve days in the hospital following surgery, eight of them in intensive care.

It was a rough ride. I cried this morning. I cried for joy. I cried out of anger. I cried for the Lisa who suffered and still suffers. I cried for the humiliation I lived through. I shrugged off 120 pounds over the past year. Hard work, that shrugging.

Last year at this time, I was lifeless, under anesthesia, a body with no ghost, a car with no driver. Last year at this time, my parents were expecting a phone call. Last year at this time, this big ol' rock was spinning and would keep on spinning no matter when that phone call came and no matter what my surgeon was going to tell them.

It's surreal to look back at the odds against me. It's unreal that I mustered the determination to save my own life. I could have died. Under the circumstances, I should have died. I refused to die in that hospital bed. It's time now.

No more living in the moldy darkness of addiction and isolation. No more staying still to avoid feeling myself shimmy and shake. No more stagnation to avoid feeling myself alive. I want more life.

August 17, 2007

LATER AND LIGHTER

I DREAMED OF THIS DAY. I wanted to *feel* better, and I do. Last year at this time, I wanted so desperately to lose even fifty pounds just to get the weight off of my sore back and sore joints. My breathing was labored. I wanted even a little relief.

I bargained with God in my head. "God, if you let me take off just fifty pounds I promise *not* to complain about how fat I still am. I promise to remember how it feels to be over four hundred pounds. I promise to remember how even losing fifty pounds seemed like a great relief. I promise to be grateful for my weight loss at every step of the way."

Then fifty pounds came off, and I complained. "Can I ever be happy just the way I am?"

Funny, I remember hating the way I looked as a teenager . . .

There I am at my half-brother's wedding with my nephew Tony. I was sixteen years old in that picture. Look at my thin, graceful arm and fingers, my pointy chin. No fat. No double chin. No age. No wrinkles. No battle scars.

Back then I *hated* the way I looked. I looked at that picture shortly after it was taken and found a hundred things wrong with it. As a forty- three-year-old looking back at this picture, I realize how beautiful I was.

So, as a forty-three-year-old, I look at the forty-three-year-old Lisa of today. How harshly I criticize myself for how I look! The harshness I felt when I was sixteen looking at the sixteen-year-old Lisa is the same harshness I feel looking at the forty-three-year-old Lisa! Years shouldn't have to pass before I can feel compassion and fondness for *who I am right now*!

My criticisms aside, I find some peace when I look at myself now, because I know how hard I worked to get here. I have newfound self-respect. I can more easily shut down that negative script, the critical self-talk in my mind, because I know that the woman in the picture, that me of the here and now, is a promise keeper, a worker—a disciplined, strong, getting-healthy woman of achievement.

I look at the pic and feel that it's not OK to say bad things about myself, not after what I've been through, not after pushing myself to go to the gym *day after day* in bad moods, good moods, lazy moods, crampy, nasty, grumpy moods and all kinds of weather (outdoor weather *and* emotional weather, oy!)

Blogging every day when last year at this time it was a major effort just to blog once a week! Once a week! Can you imagine? Weekly blogging took pushing!

And now? No, that girl, that me in the picture deserves respect. She may not be ready for the red carpet, but she's ready for flashbulbs and applause. It's OK to be OK with myself. It's appropriate to accept praise, compliments, and respect from others. It's right to be kind to myself.

Imagine what a world this would be if all the women, all the people who are drowning in illness and self-doubt, worked their way up into the light and became the light themselves. The kind people. The sensitive people. The deep, thoughtful people.

The meek *should* inherit the earth. The kind *must* inhabit the earth. Kindness begins with self. Be kind.

August 19, 2007

Clanging Monkeys

I'M STILL DEPRESSED. NOT TERRIBLY sad, but depressed.

I have to fight every damned day. My moods are raging currents that threaten to crush me into submission. The crisis of meaninglessness rises and falls like the tides drawn by the mysterious pull of an invisible moon. I'm a Leo. A fire sign. Not a moon child. Go figure.

Although depression, clinical depression, can be characterized by per- vasive feelings of sadness, despair is more often the feature that binds me. The feature that binds me, the creature that binds me, paralysis. The "why bother" feeling. The meaninglessness.

I experience manageable mania, creative mania, the "good" kind of mania that leads to house cleaning and creativity.

The dour side, the downside of my depression is bad but not too, too bad. Not suicidal. It's more of a general malaise, a "why bother" feeling, but "why bother" can be dangerous. "Why bother" ruled my life like a stark-fisted tyrant for years. Nothing mattered. Things I once enjoyed failed to excite me. The only light in my darkness was shed by my latching obsessively onto ideas, or celebrity crushes, or TV shows. The out-of- whack excitement of obsession kept me going when the day-to-day business of life failed to resonate with me.

My obsessive drives helped to fuel some amazing projects in my life, but I was physically unhealthy. I could hardly enjoy my projects and accomplishments because I couldn't stand, breathe, or walk without unbearable pain.

People who might look at me and say that the gastric bypass surgery "cured" me are not accurately assessing my condition. The surgery helped. It didn't fix everything. I still have plenty of other spinning plates to keep aloft. Having one great tool is not enough to cure me entirely, and that's all gastric bypass surgery is: one great tool. There are plenty of days where I don't think it's great at all.

I think about my health issues as if they are a room full of clanging mechanical monkeys banging their little cymbals together. OK, you got that picture in your mind? A room full of them clanging and clattering. The cacophony is unsettling.

That was the state of my health back in 2004 when I was languishing in that hospital bed, covered in staph-infected carbuncles due to out-of- control diabetes and still suffering from obstructive sleep apnea.

Clang, clang, clang, clang, clang, clang-itty clang. Who could find peace in all that racket? When I was diagnosed with apnea and started faithfully using the CPAP (I *love* my CPAP and am 100 percent compliant about using it every time I sleep, even for naps!), *one monkey shut down.* Silenced. One less set of little hairy mechanical arms clanging their tinny-sounding cymbals.

Still, I'm in a room full of clanging monkeys. Next, the diabetes monkey. He's winding down. Only a few clangs per minute at most, nearly silent.

One less monkey making noise. The depression monkey isn't clanging like windshield wipers at top speed, but he's still clanging, just not as hard, not as frequently. He's clanging more slowly now, but he clangs.

Was there a magic bullet that got me to silence my health monkeys? No. I wish there was *one* thing I could pinpoint for you, so that you could recreate it in your life. I wish there was *one* experience that changed me and set me on the right track. It doesn't work that way. There are many influences working together.

You know the old saying about how a butterfly in Africa flaps its wings and causes a hurricane in southern Florida? Not accurate. Along with the nearly insignificant flapping of the African butterfly's wings, there are a billion other teeny, tiny influences that stir up the hundred-miles-an-hour winds thousands of miles away. The butterfly's flapping does not have the huge impact that popular imagination associates with the butterfly effect. If the butterfly had not flapped its wings, the hurricane still would have happened because of the other billions of tiny influences that conspired to cause the storm. Did the butterfly's flapping contribute to the storm? Yes. Just not in a terribly significant way.

Same with my room full of monkeys. No one thing wound them up and started their clanging. No one thing will shut them down.

Are there huge, significant influences that have helped me? Sure. The bypass itself helped. The support of my friends and colleagues and students sustained me. My radically changed diet nourished me. The consistent exercise oxygenated me. My hopefulness rose as I pushed myself to keep my word. My desire to live pulled me forward. Committed action kept the momentum.

Am I depressed? Yeah. There are many days I'd rather do nothing. I'd rather not shower or clean or leave the house or buy nutritious foods for myself. I do it anyway. Why? Doing things that I don't feel like doing leads to more happiness, satisfaction, and joy. It may not feel good in the moment, but it pays off overall.

Will taking a shower right now cure my depression? No. Taking a shower, dressing, walking down the hill to the flea market in the park, going to the gym, vacuuming, and listing stuff on eBay will make me feel a notch or two higher and better than if I gave in to my inclinations to do a whole lotta nothing.

Will it bring me radical, ecstatic joy? No. It will contribute to an overall feeling of peace and satisfaction. Acting differently than I feel, resisting the depressive inclinations to marinate in my own despair by moving, acting, doing, breathing, eating good foods, keeping my word will make my monkeys just a bit quieter.

What I've learned over this past year or so is that pain avoidance is life avoidance.

Life is supposed to hurt a little. Not the way I was hurting. Not in the knees, back, ankles, lungs, and heart. Life is not supposed to hurt every time you take a breath or try to move. That's not the hurt I'm talking about.

I'm talking about the hurt of living authentically. The discomfort of facing life head on instead of cowering in the moldy darkness of addiction. Pain avoidance, issue avoidance, emotion avoidance robs us of our authenticity. We rob ourselves of our self-expression with our pain-avoidance habits. We cling to not feeling because feeling is too much to handle and then we waste away and die from our ailments. I believe our ailments are really internalized emotions that we have swept under the rug.

That lump under the rug? Look down at your body. All those avoided emotions settled there, inside you, mucus and yeasts packed into our gut along with all our undealt-with issues. I'm cleaning out my gut along with my issues, and it ain't comfortable.

Does this mean that folks who are seeking comfort are somehow defective? Hell, no! I wasn't defective back in my sick, immobile, overeating days. I was disempowered, disenchanted, disenfranchised. I was dissed. I was dissed by myself and the rest of the negative influences that conspire to rob every one of us of our very lives.

The comfort I sought was a false comfort. Ever have a cheap piece of cake? Or how about a super-cheap imitation Twinkie or cookie from the dollar store? Compare a cheap dessert to one you've had at a fancy restarant. Heck, even the desserts at Applebee's have a richness of flavor not found in your average, el cheapo, preservative-laden, budget snack cake.

The cheapo snack cake is the comfort-seeking life I was living. It looks appetizing. It seems like a good idea, but it's ultimately unfulfilling. It fails to deliver the pleasure it promises. Then it fails to nourish in a sustaining way.

Addictions are a way to avoid having to feel the painful emotions from an earlier time in our lives. Take an honest look at your past. (Warning: this could take years of difficult emotional work, but I promise the payoff is worth it.) If you're in the throes of addiction, look at your past. Something hurt you. I was hurt. Maybe it was some form of abuse, like the way I was systematically degraded by my narcissist mother. Maybe it was the constant bullying I suffered all through grammar school. Maybe it was the disappointment in my father for not rescuing me from my mother.

I have so many emotional skeletons rattling around my emotional closet, it's hard to pick one. Pick a scar, any scar. That's a clue to where it started. My failure to adequately cope with the uncomfortable emotions and express my needs in a healthy way started me on my snowballing journey of self-destruction and emotional avoidance.

I didn't express my pain. I internalized it. Then I spent most of my life trying to cover it up, like a cat in the litter box covering its poo. *Dig, dig, dig, dig, dig, scratch, scratch, scratch, scratch, scratch.* What was I left with? A giant lump of shit buried under a litter of addiction.

I don't like pushing myself to do what I don't feel like doing, but I liked my addicted life even less. It wasn't much of a life. As hard as I pushed myself to get out there in the world at about four hundred pounds the pain was almost unbearable. The rejection from men; the rejection of people in general; the sneers, insults, and unwanted advice; the finger pointing; the fist slamming against the table; the suffocating mother; the fat prejudice; the inability to move' the lack of oxygen to my brain from my sedentary life and sleep apnea; the death of my cells from diabetes; all led to the lack of hope, lack of passion, and lack of fulfillment characteristic of major depression.

Who wouldn't seek comfort under those circumstances? Fortunately, now I've decided to seek comfort in different way. I redefined "comfort" as having a life of being able to "comfortably" look at myself in the mirror, to have self-respect and integrity, to have a foundation of wellness upon which to build a life. I've lived a life where I dreaded getting out of bed in the morning. I don't want to squander my time on earth any longer. This past year, I've realized some wondrous visions. I take for granted that I can stand in the shower. It dawned on me yesterday that last year at this time I was still sitting on the tub ledge!

Last year at this time, standing in the shower was a mere wish, a vision, a dream for "someday." Walking at flea markets, walking in the supermarket, going to the gym, I wasn't able to do those things last year at this time. Three weeks after my gastric bypass, I had to return to teaching my college classes. Well, I didn't have to. I probably should have sent in a substitute for the first week or two, but I didn't. Half-dead, barely able to breathe, full of stitches, infection, fever, and crippling arthritis, I started the fall semester. My father had to drive me to school, right up to the door of University Hall. He put the flashers on and walked me up to my classroom. He held onto my left side and I groped the wall with my right. Walking from the elevator to the classroom was like running a marathon for me. As I inched forward, I had to stop and catch my breath a number of times before I reached the classroom. My father walked me to the front of the class and stayed till I was sitting at the desk and breathing regularly. Who was that girl? How did I get through that? How did I keep my faith? Back then, I imagined a time when I would be able to walk easily. I imagined a body that worked. I imagined freedom from the burden of my own body. I'm still imagining. I imagine running. I imagine working out in tight leotards. I imagine leading a movement class. I imagine going into people's homes to work them out in their beds, chairs, or sofas so they can experience that freedom for themselves. I imagine the pain gone! I imagine super-high energy, passion for what I'm doing, not wanting the day to end because I love my life so much.

August 20, 2016

Change Back

Notice how people react when you make a serious commitment to change for the better? People would rather deal with what they know, what they're used to, the predictable sameness that is nonthreatening.

Your trying to get well brings people face-to-face with their own unhealthy habits. If you stay the same, sick and sedentary, then they have a buddy, a cohort, a codependent partner in maintaining the bad habits, addictions, and old ways that have become deeply grooved into the comfort zone of their daily, safely predictable lives.

People will claw at you and try to keep you trapped in your old, destructive habits to quell their own anxiety. People don't want to be abandoned. Your new habits make them feel anxious. They may even do research to try to prove that what you are doing is unnecessary or dangerous or "not their cup of tea."

Their underlying message? "Stay the same, so I can stay the same."

The result? Stagnation, illness, death, or just the mediocre half-life of the people pleaser.

Motivational speakers like to use the "crabs in a bucket" story to demonstrate this point:

> You catch crabs by attaching some meat (often a chicken neck) to a long piece of cord and lowering it to the bottom of the bay. Crabs attach themselves to the meat and begin eating. You raise

the meat and catch the crabs in a net. Then you throw the crabs into a bucket to keep them from running around the boat and pinching people. Watch the crabs and you will see that as soon as one crab tries to escape the bucket by climbing out, the other crabs will pull it back down into the bucket.

(Joe Farcht, *Leadership Development at Its Best*)

Be prepared for people to naysay you. You want to live authentically. You want a life that's in line with *your* core beliefs and values and that's best for your health. The more you improve, the more you change, the more of a reaction you're going to get from people who try to discredit you and keep you down.

Don't give in. Be who you are. Remember, critics are expressing *their* anxiety about changing *their* lives. It's not about you.

You just keep moving forward. Be the mother duck. You know the old expression about keeping all your ducks in a row? Notice how the mother duck does that. She doesn't herd the ducklings like a sheepdog herds the sheep. She waddles forward and all the little duckies fall into line behind her. She leads. They follow. All in a row.

Don't look back. Don't worry about the ducklings. They'll either follow or die. Just *go*! The smart ones will follow.

September 13, 2007

Recovering from Dieting

I ALMOST GAVE UP THE scale for good. The reason I kept it? To teach others that weight loss is not about a daily decline in the number of pounds measured on a mechanical device. Weight fluctuates from day-to-day.

Sometimes up. Sometimes down.

The idea that something we ate yesterday has much of anything to do with the number on the scale today is false. Unless you're a binge eater like I was. Then it's true. A person can actually gain pounds in one day— pounds of food, the weight of the food sloshing around in the intestines. But those were extreme times. I don't want to carry that eating-disordered thinking into my new, healthier life, and I certainly don't want to encourage that behavior in others. The idea that if you have dessert after dinner and then have to work extra hard at the gym the next morning to burn it off is just another version of bingeing and purging. It's not healthy thinking.

Our bodies are designed for health. We just need to get out of our own way.

Restrictive dieting was a major stumbling block to my good, vibrant health. If you're dedicating too much energy to counting calories, obsessing over the scale, mulling over carbs and protein, and labeling your day as "good" or "bad" depending on what you've eaten, then you're not allowing your body to work the way it's designed to work. It's so much better to read your body's hunger cues and eat a variety of good food rather than obsess about sticking to a plan.

Same thing with exercise. It shouldn't be something you dread. My gym-going is more of a habit than a chore. For the most part I look forward to the gym. Yesterday on the stationary bike, I popped it up to level five (like pedaling uphill or in high gear), then rode while I did scratch-off lottery tickets, the crossword puzzle ones and the Bingo ones. Then I read a few pages of a book while the time flew by. I pedaled and I had fun.

September 14, 2007
No Advice, Just Story

I WANT TO LIVE MY life in such a way as to provide evidence by which other people can make decisions about their lives.

What I do wish to provide is an account of my life as one who feels disillusioned by the current system. I want my life to offer hope for those who are not recovering well using the current system. I want people to know, concretely, evidently, that there are other good options for them.

I like to avail myself of many options. My life is an example of getting well and recovering in a way that is working for me.

Detox. Transformation. Whole foods.

Lots of care.

No scale.

Self-love.

I don't think I have *the* answer, but my answer is one that's pretty damn good for me.

I'll live it and write about it, and you can judge for yourself.

September 15, 2007
OPTIONS, OPTIONS EVERYWHERE

*It makes no sense to assume that the 80 million people who are
currently dieting are somehow deficient, that they lack the discipline
to achieve something they care very much about achieving,
particularly when many of them succeed in their pursuit of goals
in other spheres of their lives. Clearly there must be something
inherent in every diet that ensures its ultimate failure.*

—JANE R. HIRSCHMANN AND CAROL H. MUNTER, *OVERCOMING OVEREATING*

I BLAMED MYSELF UP UNTIL the last minute. Right up until they put
that oxygen mask over my face in the operating room, I blamed myself
for my lack of discipline. I believed I would never be able to control my
overeating without the gastric bypass.

But what if? What if, for some reason, I was unable to have the
bypass? What would I have done? People ask me that all the time.

I'm resourceful. Better yet, I'm relentless. I was hell-bent on getting
well. I would have found a way. I might have found the best inpatient
eating disorder program and checked myself in. I might have radically
detoxed myself with internal cleansing. I may have used hypnosis and
self- talk to overcome my need to overeat. I would have bypassed the
bypass.

Don't get me wrong, it's nice to be rid of the demon. My stomach felt like a demon, no doubt about it. It growled and raged like an angry mob ready to lynch me if I didn't feed it. The hunger was unbearable, both physiological hunger and emotional hunger. My stomach was always raging at me. Without the bypass, I still would have found a way to kill it. I would have silenced the demon one way or another.

Right now it's growling a bit. One year after the surgery and I'm actually feeling hungry again. The difference is that now I'm not afraid to eat. I'm not afraid that once I start eating, I'll never stop. I trust myself to eat well and to stop when I've had enough. For the first time in my life enough *is* enough.

In the beginning, my goal was to lose weight and my deepest wish was to overcome my binge eating disorder.

I've done both.

And I'm still doing it. Still losing weight, still wrestling with my ever- weakening demon. I'm not doing it the conventional way. I don't diet. I don't count calories and I don't restrict fats.

I've made peace with chocolate cake by regarding it as one of many options available to me. The bypass assisted me in legalizing food and regarding chocolate cake as just one of many available choices.

I kinda cheated. I surgically removed eating an entire chocolate cake as an option. It's not a choice for me any longer, unless I want to make myself uncomfortably ill or rupture my stomach.

The surgery makes the decision for me. I feel like I should be suffering over the option to eat the entire cake. I should be doing the hard work of freely choosing to eat an entire cake or not. I can eat a few bites and I'm done whether I like it or not. No wrestling. No struggle. I feel like I've brought a gun to the wrestling match and shot my opponent in the knee.

Really, I *did* work hard at this. I have to keep in mind that the surgery was difficult.

The detox afterward was harrowing. I suffered. I paid my dues. Let's say I lumped my struggles, my wrestling, into those first three months of condensed misery so I wouldn't have to suffer in increments.

I don't cower under an avalanche of food to cover up my emotions. I get a light coating of snow at best. My feelings can still breathe. That's where the blogging kicks in. Blogging is an outlet for expressing my unresolved feelings.

Working out is a great way to express my emotional energy too. The gym is an outlet for anger, aggression, fear, sadness, and unfocused mania. No more pent-up energy with a bulldozer's worth of food covering it up. I sweat. I pedal. I move!

We weight-loss surgery folks had this surgery because we ran out of options (or thought we had run out of options). We were desperate. We were unable to stick with an eating regimen or diet. We wanted something drastic, something radical. Diets didn't work for us. We opted for weight- loss surgery, a surgically imposed diet. The surgery restricts us. We eat less.

When we fail to reach our goal weight or we gain back what we've lost, we slink away in shame because we "failed" at our last chance for health. We weren't good enough. We failed again and we believe it's all our fault.

Don't believe that for a second. Don't waste your thoughts on putting yourself down. Eating less works in the short-term. It always does. Diets always work in the beginning. Then our metabolism kicks in and either makes us want to eat more or slows to a crawl so we subsist on the restriction diet and hit a plateau or regain.

Maybe if we learned to eat healthy foods, a variety of pleasure foods, listened to our bodies, and moved in a fun way, our bodies would find their own best weight. I know, that's crazy talk in the weight-loss surgery world. Thin equals success. Thin equals healthy. Any other ideas are heresy.

October 5, 2007

More Life

I FEEL KINDA BEAT UP. I have aches and pains in places I didn't even know existed. I've been taking Ibuprofen or Tylenol every day. Yes, both.

That's probably not good for me.

Sometimes it hurts to stand. The bottoms of my feet flare up and stab at me. My knees pinch. These workouts are taking their toll on me. I thought about quitting. Yeah, Little Miss Motivation wants to quit. While I'm sitting here at the computer right now, my left knee is burning. There's a stinging pain in my right side. My body is stiff and achy. I feel feverish. Why am I suffering like this?

I'm getting healthy to eliminate the aches and pains, not cause more of them! What's going on?

My thoughts turn to the replicant (artificial person) Roy Batty (played by Rutger Hauer) in the movie *Blade Runner*. His time is running out. His artificial body is fading. He feels his life energy shutting down. In a fierce finale foot chase between him and Agent Deckard (Harrison Ford), we see Batty pause to look at his hand. It's going numb. He grips it in frustration, grabs a nine-inch nail, and thrusts it through his palm. He howls in agony. Why would he deliberately cause himself such pain? Because pain is something. Feeling alive, even if it's searing pain, is better than feeling nothing. If you're in pain, you're alive. He wants more life.

Should life be horribly uncomfortable and painful? No. I'm not saying that. I've been in pain for years. The discomfort of having *no* fitness level whatsoever and the pains of deterioration are not the same as my achy workout pains. One is death. The other is life.

"I want more life, f **ker," says Batty when he confronts his maker.

I want more life too. Pains and all. Maybe I'll take up some tai chi to balance out the hard-core workouts. I really don't like being in pain all the time. Shouldn't being healthier mean less pain?

I eventually beat the pain! Find out how at LisaSargese.com.

October 7, 2007

ALL OR NOTHING IS EASY

GETTING OUT OF MY COMFORT zone is not easy. Please don't read my blog as if I have it "all together" or as if I'm even *close* to being a finished product. I'll never be a finished product.

I'm not sure I'll ever have it all together. Being done once and for all is easy. Staying in flux, always striving, always changing—that's hard. When I was four hundred pounds, depressed and sedentary, I looked at fit, healthy, active folks like they had something that I didn't. They were special. They had been blessed with energy. They had it all together.

I rationalized and told myself that I was blessed with the ability to think clearly, to feel deeply, to use my brain instead of my body and that physical discomfort was the price I had to pay. I thought I deserved pain. I convinced myself of that utter nonsense.

I was convinced that some folks are designed to be well and others of us have it worse off than others. It's simply not true. My big, fat ass was just as movable as the fit, small Lycra-clad asses I saw jogging in the early morning or dancing on TV with a bare midriff. I had it in me. I just didn't know it yet.

On an intellectual level, I knew it. I knew that I was physically able to get up off my ass, stretch, walk (or do the "walk and plop," since I couldn't walk more than a few yards without excruciating pain) to start slowly and build up my fitness level.

But, on a deep level, I thought I was doomed. I didn't really believe I could do it. So I stayed doomed. I believed I was stuck in a self-destructive loop of misguided self-soothing (overeating) that would be impossible to break without bypass surgery. My beliefs created my reality. I had the surgery. I got out of the self-destructive loop.

Yesterday, I was garage saleing with my mother. We pulled up to a driveway just as the wind was knocking over a clothing rack in front of a small, frail older woman. She backed away from the killer clothes rack without being hurt. I jumped out of the car, asked if she was OK, and helped her pick up the clothes from the driveway. Her daughter-in-law thanked me a million times over for helping. We got to talking.

The daughter-in-law had just lost sixty-eight pounds. I asked her secret. "I stopped eating," she said.

She told me she had considered the bypass surgery but was denied by insurance. She was determined to do it "on her own." I told her to take heart. She could do it on her own. I told her that the surgery doesn't guarantee success, that it kinda stops working after a few months and forces the patient to do it "on her own" anyway. I told her that I totally transformed my eating. I told her that I went to the gym six days a week. She nodded, then she said it again. "I just stopped eating."

I didn't want to get into a debate with her about how wrongheaded that was. Stopping eating is not a healthy way to live. We have to eat to live. I don't think starving is the way to be healthy. We are fuel-burning machines. We need food.

I've been really "mouthy" (mouth hungry as opposed to stomach hungry) over the past thirty-six hours, craving carby foods: cereal, whole-wheat pasta, bread. What is going on? I don't know what my body is trying to tell me.

Well, one way to decipher that would be to say I'm a "carbohydrate addict" and then punish myself mentally for being "weak." I could deny my cravings and let myself go hungry. It takes willpower to not eat when you're hungry, right? Willpower means we're disciplined and therefore "good," right?

Or, I could eat the foods I crave and think of it in an empowering way. Think about it. Why was I craving certain foods? Did my body need the nutrients in those foods? Did my body need the iron? The calories? The easy-to-digest fuel? I think eating what my body craves and letting it do with it what it wants is the best option. That sounds like crazy talk for people who have surgery to defeat their cravings. Eating what we crave sounds indulgent, so we resist the idea.

"I stopped eating" doesn't sound like the mantra of a person who is on a healing track. "I stopped eating" is not the credo of someone who has learned to love her body and embrace her physical and emotional needs. Hunger isn't weakness. Hunger is the expression of a legitimate need. Cravings might be the expression of very specific needs.

It takes character, integrity, strength, and compassion to take the middle path. The all-or-nothing approach of "I stopped eating" doesn't create healthy habits. It's unnatural. It's drastic. It's anorectic. It's restraining. It's denial at its worst. It's denying that we have the ability to learn to be at peace with our needs.

We should learn to have a peaceful relationship with food. We need food to survive. We need good food in order to thrive. Why do we hear so much about weight-loss surgery and not eating disorder recovery? Why is weight-loss surgery so much in the public conversation but recovery is not?

The noneating garage-sale woman looked at me as we spoke. "How many kids do you have?" she asked.

"I have four cats. Ha ha! No kids. Never married," I answered. She looked like she felt sorry for me.

"You're how old, about my age? About fifty, right?" she asked.

I hoped I didn't sound too defensive when I corrected her. She thanked me again for helping her mother-in-law with the flying clothes rack. She gave me a generous discount on the hefty bag of clothes I bought from her.

I grabbed all of her husband's old Aéropostale T-shirts for fifty cents each. I was happy with my bargain but perplexed by her "I stopped eating" remark. I almost felt guilty about my commitment to feeding myself in a healthy way.

This extreme view of abstinence as an all-or-nothing proposition doesn't seem right to me. Being hungry and making the tough choice to cook, prepare, or get off our asses and go buy the good food our bodies need at the moment takes work. For someone with an eating disorder, it takes bravery. For someone who isn't used to taking care of one's self, it's radical.

October 8, 2007

Yank the Vision

If you don't take control of your life, don't complain when others do.

—Beth Mende Conny, *The Art of Schmooze*

I know that vague visions bring vague results. Knowing it doesn't help me yank my vision into focus. It just makes me feel guilty for not knowing exactly what I want.

Star, my one-thousand-year-old (OK, more like somewhere in her late 80s) psychic, whom I see twice a year at the Save the Animals Rescue Team's Tricky Tray events, read my cards last Sunday. According to Star, things are looking better for me health-wise. I need a kick in the pants career-wise. She dealt the cards and read them. She saw my future. She saw me talking, something involving talking to groups. She saw me in front of a room full of people. "They're depressed," she said, "and you're going to help them."

My eyes teared up a bit. I was a little choked up. She saw it more clearly than I did. Her vision made me want to cry. Having faith in my talents is still new to me.

Deep down, I know what I have to do. I need to get in front of the room and talk. I've watched many motivational speakers, trainers, consultants, and teachers in my lifetime. They seem special. They have a star quality, but when the spotlight is turned off and they're mingling with us common folk, they lose their luster. They're just people after all.

They're people with stories, people who struggled, people who made some discoveries. They talk about it. They get paid. So what's stopping me? Something must be stopping me. It's always the same answer: fear. The mind killer. The little death.

I'm afraid people won't want to listen to me because I'm still fat. I'm afraid I'll be tired. I'm afraid I won't want to do it once I start. I'm afraid no one will want to hear what I have to say.

We all know the true meaning of courage, right? Courage isn't the absence of fear. Courage is being afraid and doing it anyway. I'm afraid to move forward on this, but I'm doing it anyway. Getting healthier frightens me, but I'm doing it anyway. Losing weight terrifies me, but I'm doing it anyway. I may not be jumping headfirst into the water with one giant splash, but I'm slowly dipping my feet in. I'd say I'm wet up to the knee.

I'm afraid to be attractive. I'm uncomfortable with attention from men. I don't trust them, and I don't trust myself around them. It's understandable. Many men have been unkind to me all my life. They've been critical, harsh, judgmental, and disingenuous. I let them treat me that way. In my desperation for their attention and approval, I've allowed them to say and do terrible things to me. They've cheated on me, stolen from me, and put me down. They've used me and gotten me into trouble. The stories of what I tolerated could fill a book, and they will. Lied to, cheated on, used, and verbally abused. They mistreated me, and I allowed them to mistreat me. I figured I deserved it. I figured I was fat and unworthy. I should be grateful for any tiny bit of anything these ne're-do-wells were willing to toss my way. They systematically wore me down, treated me like a nonperson, and since I was used to feeling that way, I accepted the treatment.

The result? Not so trusting of men. Go figure.

So, yeah, I'm not anxious to put myself out there speaking-career-wise or dating-wise. I want to toughen up. I want to learn to draw healthy boundaries. I want to have self-respect and get respect from others. I guess that's a clear goal, right?

I need to yank my vision into a clearer shape.

October 9, 2007

"Someday" Never Comes

TIME ERASES THE "NOW" AND turns it into "then" without our consent. Time erases importance.

I was twenty-seven once. I turned forty-three without any warning. That's how time works. It's relentless. While we're procrastinating and fooling ourselves into thinking we have a million tomorrows to handle our problems, time is advancing, steadily, invincibly, until it runs us over when we've turned our backs on it.

I could have cowered against life till it ran me over and killed me. I chose differently. It ran me over, but I lived.

Good thing I didn't want to turn forty. Good thing I turned forty-one and hated that even more. Thank God that at forty-two I panicked and turned my life around. The magic number forty woke me up. Stunned me into wakefulness. *I am mortal!* Praise God that at forty-three, I still have a self to love.

It could have gone the other way. I've watched people die without doing what they thought they would do "eventually." That could have been me. Eventually, I was going to lose weight. Eventually, I was going to clean up my eating habits. Eventually, I was going to exercise and get in shape.

"Eventually" never happens. Trust me, I know.

I figured that my wanting to do something about my life would eventually make me do something. As long as those big, important things were on my to-do list, they'd get done one of these days. "One of these days" never comes. "Someday" never arrives. I turned forty without "someday" coming. I hit forty-one and "someday" hadn't miraculously materialized out of my vague desire for it.

I had to make it. With my own resolve I had to declare it. Resolve created my "someday" and made it real. I must *never* forget that lesson. I'm tempted to wait again. I'm getting comfortable and getting the "someday" feeling. Someday, I'll write my book. Someday, I'll get my resume in order and apply for another teaching job. Someday, I'll get the cosmetic surgery to put my body back together. Someday, I'll get this knee taken care of.

I've been waiting to be ready. I've been hoping to be able to trust myself with what I've done so far before taking more risks. Here's a bold declaration: I trust my habits. I trust my *new* habits. Or do I?

I want to add more. Hear that, self? You can add more. I don't want to turn fifty with my "somedays" still in me.

Here my convictions:

I believe that our bodies are innately intelligent. They tell us what they need in the form of cravings. We crave sugar, flour, fried foods, and junk foods because our bodies want easy-to-assimilate calories.

Our healthy, brilliant bodies are more apt to hold onto weight (fat) than they are to let it go.

Survival, that wonderful programming that keeps our bodies alive, prepares us for possible famine by holding onto fat. Our bodies "like" staying the same weight. Our bodies "like" to burn calories rather than burn fat.

Therefore . . .

I've been stuck in the 250s because I've been feeding my body's needs. I've been listening to my body and answering its needs by feeding it. My body has been wanting carbs. I've been craving brown rice, Wasa, whole-grain cereal, oat bran bagels, whole-wheat pasta, and so on. I guess my body needs the fuel—easy-to-use fuel.

I've been feeding myself on demand—good, applause, wonderful, overcoming that binge-purge cycle, brava!—by listening to my body's needs and feeding it without guilt. My body is *brilliant* (so is yours), and I *love* it for working so well.

It takes focus and discipline to acknowledge hunger and honor it without judgment. It takes a radical self-love to feed that hunger in a caring, conscious way. It takes willpower to shut out the voices that say a fat person doesn't "deserve" to eat. Eating with awareness rather than judgment leads to freedom. Making choices rather than restricting entire food groups leads to peace of mind and body.

These words mean a lot to me. The way things are said makes all the difference in how I feel and behave.

October 12, 2007

PROGRESS

*Most people when they stop dieting and scolding themselves for eating
are surprised to find that life is much easier than they anticipated.*

—JANE R. HIRSCHMANN AND CAROL H. MUNTER, *OVERCOMING OVEREATING*

LIFE WAS EASIER YESTERDAY. I was barely hungry. Yeah, I still have those
days when I feel like eating less makes me virtuous.

I picked at the food in my lunch box. At the end of the day, the lunch
box was almost as full and heavy as when I packed it in the morning. I
must resist the urge to call myself "good" for not eating too much. I must
learn to regard my hunger and my eating to satisfy it with no judgment.

It's amazing what can happen when we give ourselves permission to
eat. There was a time when I believed having too much food in front of
me or in my fridge or on my shelves meant I would surely gobble it all up
in an anxious binge. I've proven to myself that this is not a true story. I
don't have to be the person who gobbles it all up just because it's in front
of me. I can be at peace with a full cupboard.

In *Overcoming Overeating*, Hirschmann and Munter advise carrying a
food bag, so we can provide ourselves with food whenever and wherever
we need it. Feeding ourselves when we're hungry establishes self-trust.
We diminish our anxiety around our neediness. We get hungry, we eat,

we feel taken care of. We heal. Don't mention this in an online forum of weight-loss surgery folks. You'll be banished.

For most of my life, abundance made me anxious. If there was food in front of me, I feared I'd never be full. I believed I would eat and eat and eat, and I'd never feel satisfied. I feared if I provided food for myself that I would eat and eat and eat till I passed out. This was a well-grounded fear. I did eat and eat and eat till I passed out, every day, for most of my adult life. My fear matched my story about myself and that matched my behavior.

Why should today be any different from yesterday? But today *is* different than yesterday. My old story about me being a glutton no longer applies. A story loses its power once we stop telling it. Writing this blog is my way (one of my ways) of telling a *new*, empowering story about who I am. The new, better story matches my new, better me.

Some folks dig their fingernails into me with their nasty comments, scold me, tell me I'm too rebellious or delusional or whatever. I'm tempted to listen to them. They're evidence is compelling. I'm still fat after all that. Little by little, I'm toughening up. People's comments (by "comments," I mean the negative, fat-shaming comments people leave me here on my blog) might get to me, but they don't stop me on my quest for wholeness. The negative voices have their say, but I let the positive comments (the wonderful, generous, uplifting comments that help me persevere) become my truth instead. That's progress.

If I were truly enlightened, neither positive nor negative comments would have an effect on me, but hey, I'm not the frickin' Buddha!

Last night, I gave a talk in a graduate class to students getting their teacher certification (or MA in education). I had spoken to many of them in a previous class. One student asked me how much weight I had lost since he had seen me speak in July.

I panicked a bit. "Not much" is the answer. I think I've lost ten pounds or so in the past four months. The weight loss has slowed down.

I felt ashamed. I felt guilty. Here I am giving motivational talks on how I changed my life, and my life seems like it's at a standstill because the weight loss is at a standstill.

Time to read my post about "someday" never coming and remind myself that four months will pass whether I make something happen or not. Wouldn't it be nice if four months from now I had something *big* to show for it? Drastic weight loss is the crowd pleaser these days.

There was a time in my life when the only thing I did every day was overeat. That's changed. I do good, positive things every day. I make commitments. I keep my word. And it's a big deal.

In my wanting to get to the next level, I must learn to include pride, satisfaction, and acknowledgement for what I've already done. Keep the story positive. Keep it real, my version of real, ya know?

October 20, 2007

HARD TO LOVE

I have tried and I cannot find either in scripture or history, a strong-willed individual whom God used greatly until He allowed them to be hurt deeply.

—CHARLES SWINDOLL

THE NEUROPATHY IS BAD THIS morning. My hands burn, then go numb, then tingle, then ache. It doesn't happen often, maybe once a week. When the diabetes was worse, the neuropathy kicked up a few times a day, painfully. Since the diabetes is improving, so is the neuropathy.

It feels like residual pain from my session with hypnosis. A few nights ago, I was the subject in a past-life regression. Well, I was supposed to regress into a past life, but instead I went back to my childhood. Since then, I've been more aware of how much I don't like five-year-old Lisa. Maybe I can love her, but I can't seem to like her.

A friend, who was at the hypnosis meeting and witnessed my emotionally expulsive session, e-mailed me an article. He thought it might help me with the hard work of parenting Little Lisa.

He suggested I reach out to healthier people for the love, acceptance, and nurturing that I craved as a child but didn't receive. Like the love I wanted from my broken, haunted, screwed-up mother. She never understood me. I rarely felt appreciated. I knew she loved me, but she resented me too. I was supposed to be an extension of her. My job was to make her feel good about herself. When I tried to be my own original, authentic self, I was shamed for it. Our personalities kinda solidify at age five. That would be the age when her disgust of me began. No wonder I have a hard time loving Little Lisa.

Wow. That's an incredible insight. And all this time I thought my relationship problems were because of my relationship with my father. He's another one. He loves me. I have no doubt about that. He *never* hit me. Never. But when he tried to stand up to my mother for being overly critical of me or just downright cruel, he gave up too easily. Her verbal attacks were too cutting and personal, and like the typical victim of abuse, I would cringe and hope he wouldn't upset her too much or else she'd take it out on me the next day.

If I hid behind him or took his side (his side equaling his sticking up for me and questioning why she had to be so hard on me or why she had to hit me right in front of him), she would make me pay for it the next time he left the house or when he went to work. I'd get the silent treatment or she'd refuse to drive me somewhere I needed to go.

Little Lisa was stuck at home with the angry, abusive mother who made me think that *her* moods were all my fault. She would tell me I was ungrateful and spiteful for taking my father's side against her in a fight. She'd say overly dramatic things like, "Things will never be the same again—not after last night. You defied your mother!"

I had no peace. Even going to school didn't help. I was bright, I participated in class, I got high grades, but I had a quirky personality. I didn't spend time with kids my age, so I wasn't socialized. I was nerdy and awkward. I stood out. The kids picked on me. I was taunted, made fun of, and, once in a while, beat up. I dreaded stepping onto the playground every day, then I dreaded coming home.

I had no escape. I was tormented at home, tormented at school, and made to feel guilty when anyone was kind to me or defended me. No wonder I developed an eating disorder. No wonder Little Lisa is so hard to love. Who loved her?

I've been using food as emotional Spackle, trying desperately to fill in the cracks of my broken childhood since childhood! But when

I imagine Little Lisa, it's hard to have sympathy for her. She's so eager to please an unpleasable mother that she's become a little version of her: broken, needy, socially unpredictable, and hard to love. She wants to be herself, but she's afraid. I associate her fear with cowardice, yet it was self-preservation. I was trying to hard to protect myself, yet I was pathetic and often unlikeable.

My God, how will I ever heal from all this? Binge eating all these years has postponed coming face-to-face with what I lived through. It's buried my feelings of sadness, rage, and shame. Now, without the binge eating, I'm feeling it all. I'm remembering.

So much work to be done. I have to believe that I'm worth it.

October 21, 2007

Attracting Blessings

I'VE BEEN HOVERING IN THE low 250s for months. Months! I should be frustrated by now, right?

Well, I am a little bit frustrated. But—and everybody loves a big *but*— I'm not discouraged.

I'm making progress even if the scale isn't dipping dramatically. My body is changing. I feel it in my waist. I feel it down my sides. There's no denying it. I'm shrinking. I'm letting go of the protective layer of fat.

I looked in the mirror at the gym yesterday while I was weight training. I liked my reflection. I've made progress. I am stronger. I see it. I feel it. I am pleased with myself. Just being pleased with myself is something new. It's huge progress.

So, I'm at the gym and just as I was radiating that feeling of pride, a young man came over to me. He saw that I had been struggling to pop some widget into place on the pectoral fly machine. He helped me. It was a spontaneous act of kindness. I was grateful. I'm always so surprised when anyone's kind to me.

There was another spontaneous, kind act that showed up in my life on Friday. It was pouring rain. My mother and I went to Best Buy to get her a new boombox (yes, my eighty-four-year-old mother needed a new boombox). I warned her that Best Buy is *huge* and that she'd have a hard time walking through the store.

As we walked into the store, near the entrance we saw two public wheelchairs next to the shopping carts. In the past, my mother had never warmed up to the idea of letting me push her in a wheelchair, no matter how I reassured her that it didn't make her an invalid. This time, out of necessity, she relented. Not even relented, she suggested it.

I worried that I wouldn't be strong enough to push her around the store. Turns out, pushing her was easy. I guess all that working out and building my body has paid off, no matter what the scale says!

We had fun. In the middle of the store, without warning, my mother came out with, "Dee, dee, dee," her take on the Carlos Mencia bit. The two of us laughed so hard we were turning heads. I was doubled over laughing. We were downright silly.

We finished shopping. I wheeled her through the checkout and into the vestibule. It was pouring rain outside. There was no way for me to hold the umbrella over the both of us and push the wheelchair at the same time. I told her to hold the umbrella over herself. "Don't worry, Ma," I reassured her. "If I get wet, I won't melt."

We arranged our purchase on her lap. She held the umbrella over herself and her lap full of electronic goodies as I pushed her to the car. I was fully exposed to the rain like the ever dutiful, self-sacrificing daughter.

But I wasn't getting wet. For a split second, I thought I was miraculously walking between the raindrops. I looked up. There as an umbrella over my head. A woman, who later told us she was a Baptist, was following us, holding an umbrella over my head and her own as she followed close behind.

"Mmmm, you two ladies are sure having a good time," she remarked.

I just kept saying thank you over and over again. She stayed, holding that umbrella over us while I packed the car and got my mother inside.

"God bless you," she said as she walked away. Yes. God had blessed us with her salvific act of compassion. Out of the rain, someone thought I deserved to be sheltered.

I bet the laughing had a lot to do with it. Just like I believe my sudden burst of radiant self-confidence brought that young man over to help me at the gym, our joyful spirits attracted the kindness of that woman in the middle of the pouring rain.

There's something about energy. Certain energy attracts certain things.

I won't put out frustrated, negative energy regarding my current state of health. I'm resisting the urge to be discouraged over this weight-loss plateau. It's not even a real plateau, because I *feel* my body changing. I'm thankful that for the first ten months after the surgery I lost an average of two pounds per week. If that has changed, and now I'm averaging half a pound a week, so be it.

I'm reaping too many other rewards that "outweigh" the numbers on the scale.

When I'm spending time with my mother, despite my anger over incidents from my childhood, I'm able to enjoy her for who she is, and we have a good time. I won't let the bad memories prevent me from making new, happy memories.

October 29, 2007

Clean Up

I HAD A PRODUCTIVE DAY. Started the day with movement. Took a walk later in the day. Cleaned!

I finally got the broken glass out of the corner. A glass display case that held a few of my smaller collectibles (a miniature frog from my Grandma Wittig, Mrs. Potts and Chip, a tiny Death Star) had fallen off a high shelf and shattered on my bedroom floor I dunno how many months ago. When it first happened, I picked up the larger shards of glass and left the broken case in the corner where the beloved miniatures waited to be rescued from a dangerous maze of jagged glass.

I procrastinated every time I looked in the corner where it sat menacingly. I told myself:

"I'll do it when I have the energy. It's not a priority; other stuff needs to be done. I'll get to it when I have time. It's safely contained in the corner, away from the cats, so I can put off cleaning it up indefinitely. One of these days I'll get to it."

Yesterday was that day. I had the energy. As a matter of fact, yesterday was the day I put away a few different stuffed-into-the-corner things that had been low priorities for months, like the paperweight I received as a graduation present last June. I spent four months pretending the gift bag wasn't there every time I passed it. I convinced myself it didn't matter that it was taking up space in the corner. Geez, so much denial. What kind of energy does that take?

I knew where I was going to put certain things: the top cabinet above my sink. So, it's not like I didn't have a plan for that bag of stuff. I did have a plan, but I dreaded going through with it. Reaching the top cabinet would require standing on something. I wasn't in a hurry to do that. Effort, pain, and exertion surely awaited me. There was no other way to reach that top cabinet. I had to climb.

I had a choice. I could either stand on a kinda high stool that I sometimes sit on (near the stove and sink or when feeding the cats) or I could lug the stepladder from behind my closet door in my bedroom. The step-ladder would inevitably be draped with giant tumbleweeds of dust that had to be removed before I could even attempt to bring it into the kitchen. Which would it be, a kinda high stool or a dusty stepladder?

I chose the stool (though I did get the tumbleweeds off the ladder when I cleaned up the glass-shard explosion in the bedroom). Using the stool turned out to be a magnificent triumph. I did the one-leg-step-up while holding onto the sink ledge for support. Wow. It was amazing. I felt so nimble!

There are more payoffs from working out than just the numbers on a scale. I stood on a stool. That's a huge payoff. My neater apartment is a huge payoff too. All clothes have been sorted, folded, and put away. I even got rid of a handful of mismatched socks and a few things that no longer fit (hallelujah).

Little things that seem so mundane make a huge difference. Having suffered from depression most of my life, I can tell you how hard it is to care for myself. Taking care of paperwork, paying bills, keeping a clean house, feeding myself well, keeping up with daily disciplines are not as easy for a clinical depressive as they are for nondepressed folks.

Depression is more than just a "bad mood." It's a persistent state of hopelessness caused by a chemical imbalance. I'm not taking that from any website definition, though you can find plenty of helpful stuff online that describes clinical depression and its symptoms. I understand and can name this state of hopelessness, apathy, and meaninglessness because I have lived it and sometimes still do live it.

Do I believe depression can be cured? Sure! Body chemistry can change. The subconscious can be cleaned out. Minds, bodies, and souls can heal no matter how broken. Like I said, I'll never stop working on myself. Self-care. Yeah. That's a big issue with me. Yesterday was a major care-for-Lisa day. Walking around my freshly vacuumed apartment without tripping over piles of dirty clothes and other unsorted crap is a testament to my ability to care for myself. It makes me feel like I'm worth the effort. I've added a brick to a foundation of self-trust. I feel lighter, more optimistic, abler.

The living-space upkeep goes hand in hand with eating better, exercising regularly, daily disciplines, and overall moves toward wellness. Healing from a behavioral disorder (in my case, a binge eating disorder) requires an integrative approach. Just the surgery wouldn't have done it. Just the exercise wasn't going to do it. Just eating less wasn't what I needed. I needed to improve my relationship with food, improve the quality of foods in my life, get moving and oxygenated, and work on my undealt-with emotions. All these aspects have to work together in order for a person to be well.

We should feel what we feel without judging ourselves. Judgment always landed me in a cycle of blame and made me even more sick and sedentary. We should choose to feel what we feel as we feel it. Choosing keeps me moving.

I can eat well. I can move. I can do good things for myself. I can act. I can choose better thoughts.

November 10, 2007

Rehab

I TRIED YOGA AT HOME. I figured without the pressure of having to do it in front of a group, I could take my time and really do the poses the correct way. I was wrong.

It seems that my body actually gets in the way of doing certain poses (asanas). I'm too big and wiggly in certain areas. My legs are too wide and short. My abs hang and actually get in my way. I'm not strong enough to hold the poses for very long.

Doing the simplest pose (upward-facing dog) actually hurt. My arms burned. My torso shook with the exertion of it. It didn't just hurt, it made me want to vomit. I'm not exaggerating. I did upward-facing dog and felt like puking.

Doing yoga alone didn't give me the freedom I'd hoped for. It gave me the freedom to feel things more authentically, but the authentic feeling turned out to be nausea. Go figure.

I'm discouraged. (Not defeated, there's a difference.) I've been working out for almost a year and I'm still terribly out of shape. I feel weak. My joints hurt. I get out of breath too easily. Working out hard means I have to nap harder.

It made me realize what the next leg of this journey is about: *rehabilitation.*

When I hear the word "rehab," I think of celebrities recovering from drug addiction. I think of junkies sitting in a circle during group therapy wishing they were high rather than having to sit on a hard chair listening to other people's stories. I think of bad coffee and powdered nondairy creamer in a church basement. Cigarettes and diet soda. 12-step programs. That's not the rehab I'm talking about. It's about rebuilding myself.

It's about coming back to life from the inside out.

Waking up the tired muscles. Getting the rest of the weight off. Nourishing myself.

Putting my body back in place. Healing from disordered eating. Taming destructive urges and emotional addictions. Becoming an expert at self-care so it becomes effortless.

I like to imagine that I'm in a helping profession. How can I take care of anyone else if I'm half-dead? Me first. I have to put myself first. That phrase is hard to digest. We resist it. We're taught that we're supposed to make our lives about others. But we forget what Jesus said: "Love your neighbor as thyself."

If we ain't loving the self, we sure ain't loving the neighbors. The world needs us to be healthy. We need ourselves to be healthy. I need myself to be healthy.

After almost forty years of destructive habits, I've damaged myself. One year of becoming better at self-care isn't going to magically fix all that damage. It takes more than a year to turn a demilitarized zone into a green, thriving neighborhood.

So why the yoga?

There are asanas that I can do without feeling like I'm falling apart. I will do them. Simple asanas are the place to start without guilt, without judgment that I should be doing more, without pressure. Even simple asanas can help me gain balance. You'd be surprised at the focus and strength it takes to be in mountain pose.

Looks like she's just standing there, right? Wrong. This is a disciplined pose. With focus and intention, you press down into the ground with your feet standing with your big toes touching. Think that's easy for me? It ain't. My muscles twitch. My body sways. I have to struggle to stay balanced.

Standing there with toes touching and feet pressing into the ground, lift the muscles in the thighs—not moving the thighs, just being aware of those big thigh muscles and feeling them lifting the body upright as the feet press down into the ground.

At this point, I'm supposed to be breathing through my nose. I'm out of breath. I have to breathe with my mouth open. Shoulders down, butt tucked in, spine nice and elongated like a string of pearls reaching toward the sky. Still teetering. Swaying on my feet. Keeping balance is work.

Maybe these simple moves are easy for some people. God bless 'em.

Let them do more advanced work. I don't need to keep up with anyone but myself.

I'm acknowledging that I have recovery work to do. Going from 400 pounds down to my current 250 has changed my body drastically. No wonder I hit a plateau! My body needs to recover. It needs care. It needs balance. It needs nourishment. It needs love.

You know I'm a fighter. I won't settle for this current state of fitness. I'm going to push onward. I woke up this morning in pain from the damp, cold weather. Everything hurt. I creaked and groaned my way out of bed. Knowing what I know, I had to move if I was going to change my sluggish stiffness. I didn't want to. I wanted to take a painkiller and go back to bed.

Lying down and snuggling in under the covers may have felt good at the moment, but it would not have given me the energy I needed to get through my morning. I forced myself to breathe. I pushed myself to do mountain pose. I raised my arms to the ceiling and looked up. That little bit of moving and stretching brought me out of my morning funk. It's a start.

I'll do what I can until I can do more. Breaking the cycle of addiction takes more willpower than just saying, "No, thank you" to a piece of chocolate cake.

I love the first year of my story so far. Last night, my best buddy described it as boot camp. He also pointed out that being a marine requires coming out of boot camp and using those skills to actually do something in the world. Boot camp is the beginning. Being a marine requires living and being courageous out in the world.

Last year at this time, I was looking for something. I found it. I wanted discipline. I developed it. I wanted motivation. I created it. I wanted to be born again hard and I did it.

This past year was incredible. As my buddy pointed out, I proved to myself and the world that I could do it. Now, as is appropriate for a seeker, explorer, thinker, and healer like me, I need something new, the next leg of my journey.

I'm standing at the crossroads, making my decision, coming up with my next move.

I'll never settle. I'll never stop.

Afterword

I FINALLY BROKE THAT PLATEAU. After the first year or two after weight loss surgery, many people hit a brick wall. I was stuck at my brick wall for a while, but I busted through it, NOT by eating less and exercising more. Nope. What I did might surprise you, but first, I landed myself in a wheelchair. I spent two years as a roller-goddess before having two total knee replacements, studying Qi Gong for healing and manifesting, and creating YouTube videos to help other people get through their own brick walls.

Told ya I'd never stop!

My story isn't over. I'm living it and I'm still telling it.

Find me on Instagram, Facebook, Twitter, and Tumblr for daily insights and inspiration so you can feel healthy and free!

Learn to Love Your Body and Be Your Healthiest Self Using the Exact System Lisa Uses...All for FREE

Do you struggle with your resolutions to get healthy and love yourself? Have you tried and failed at motivational techniques, positive thinking, and building will power?

I share my solution with you for free in a powerful video I've created just for you. Get it here: LisaSargese.com.

I understand your pain because I've had the same struggles. Which is why I'd love to share with you the system I discovered that enabled me to not only finally lose 140 pounds, but also to learn how to really love myself and develop true health.

It's all in the video, which is yours for free.

Get it now at: LisaSargese.com

Find me on Instagram, Facebook, Twitter, and Tumblr for daily insights and inspiration so you can feel healthy and free!

About the Author

LISA REMEMBERS, AT SIX YEARS old, hiding in her grandmother's kitchen and eating six meatballs in under a minute. Placed on restrictive diets beginning in kindergarten, she was continually sneak eating and binge eating as a child, partially out of rebellion, mostly because she was hungry all the time. After years of yo-yo dieting, binge eating and purging as a teen, and reaching nearly four hundred pounds as  an adult, Lisa sought out her first weight loss surgery at age twenty-three. She soon discovered that weight loss surgery isn't the easy way out. Lisa's book, *Diary of a Fat Girl* documents her first year after gastric bypass, her third in a series of weight loss surgeries that didn't work. She blogged every day as she unraveled the pain of her past and told, in painful detail, what it's like to recover from a severe eating disorder. Every year of her blog will be turned into new, inspiring books. Look for them on Amazon, Kindle, and Audible.

Made in the USA
Monee, IL
02 December 2019